Steel Ships,
Iron Crosses,
and
Refugees

STEEL SHIPS, IRON CROSSES,

— AND —

REFUGEES

*The German Navy in
the Baltic, 1939–1945*

CHARLES W. KOBURGER, JR.

New York
Westport, Connecticut
London

Library of Congress Cataloging-in-Publication Data

Koburger, Charles W., Jr.
   Steel ships, iron crosses, and refugees : the German Navy in the
Baltic, 1939–1945 / Charles W. Koburger, Jr.
      p.   cm.
   Bibliography: p.
   Includes index.
   ISBN 0–275–93260–5 (alk. paper)
   1. Germany. Kriegsmarine—History—World War, 1939–1945.
2. World War, 1939–1945—Naval operations, German. 3. World War,
1939–1945—Campaigns—Baltic Sea Region.   I. Title.
D772.3.K62   1989
940.54'5943—dc19   89–3871

Library of Congress Catalog Card Number: 89–3871
ISBN: 0–275–93260–5

First published in 1989

Praeger Publishers, One Madison Avenue, New York, NY 10010
A division of Greenwood Press, Inc.

Printed in the United States of America

The paper used in this book complies with the
Permanent Paper Standard issued by the National
Information Standards Organization (Z39.48–1984).

10 9 8 7 6 5 4 3 2 1

For Marga
from one author to another

Contents

Illustrations

TABLES

MAPS

Introduction

As World War II drew to a close, Germany's Third Reich was being driven in upon itself, made to give up all of the conquests of Hitler's black empire. Sometimes, as the Allies exacted retribution, the combatants seemed to descend to a last frenzy of killing. The *Götterdämmerung* had arrived bringing terrible devastation. (Witness the Allied bomb-generated firestorm of 1945 in Dresden.)

Another drawn-out frenzy was running its course in the Baltic (*Ostsee*, in German). There, millions of desperate civilian refugees, wounded troops, and combat units struggled westward on land and by sea for most of a year, fighting to escape the all-consuming maw of the vengeful Russians. While we may indeed have heard about Dresden, regarding this last the West seems little aware.

As in the middle thrashed an already mortally wounded Nazi state, the Reich, nonetheless, managed to carry out the largest amphibious lift—an evacuation of refugees, wounded, and troops under fire, by sea—in the history of the world.

Not all those brought out were innocent Germans. Unavoidably there were also small numbers of SS, Baltic collaborators, local nationalists, and anticommunists, all those who feared the oncoming Russians more than leaving their homes and risking the unknown perils of flight. This would all get sorted out later.

In the process of this *Götterdämmerung* the German *Volk* suffered two of the largest maritime losses in recorded history. At 6000 dead for each ship, nothing in our own past even comes near them. The only U.S. disaster to approach this scale of destruction is the little known case of the Transport *Sultana* in 1865: 2,300 people perished when the ship caught fire on the Mississippi near Memphis.

We all know of *Titanic* (lost in 1912 to an iceberg; 1500 dead) and *Lusitania* (lost in 1915 to a U-boat; 1200 dead). Both together, however, total less than half the losses on either of the German ships.

British transport *Lancastria's* loss to *Luftwaffe* dive bombers off Saint Nazaire in 1940 is possibly less well known. At perhaps 3500 dead, the British loss was considered so disastrous that details were not released until after the war's conclusion.

Should we not know more about this great German humanitarian effort? We know all about the Holocaust and, more parochially, about the U-boats and the surface raiders. To maintain our perspective, shouldn't we know about the Baltic rescue, too? Prisoners of our home culture, few of us do.

The German Navy (*Kriegsmarine*) had by 1944 been fighting in the Baltic for five years. It played a leading role in the next year's rescue operations, once again showing what a navy is for. To the *Kriegsmarine*, the war began and ended here. It was only the last year, however, that showed what a well led and adequately trained force can achieve, even if without air support and in confined waters, against a powerful but poorly led enemy.

The German Navy pulled off this truly stupendous evacuation, succeeding in the face of almost impossible odds. It took naval control of shipping, managed it, covered it, and brought it home. Its losses were not more than they had to be. The story is an epic one.

In the process the *Kriegsmarine* found a positive, historic self-image for itself. A navy long without a positive tradition—submarines, raiders, and scuttlings do not such a tradition make—it established one in the Baltic in 1944-1945. As others have noted, ships can be built much easier and even quicker than can a true fighting fleet.

The German Merchant Marine (*Handelsmarine*) played what technically was a supporting role in these operations. But here its role was so extensive and so critical to the enterprise's success that traditional lines of demarcation between it and the Navy soon acquired little meaning. Its personnel died along with those of the fighting ships. Sea service personnel were in many cases simply assigned where they would be of most use. Few were found wanting.

What is there for us in all this? Aside from the interest in reading another history of the human adventure, the critical role played by sea power—and a merchant marine as one necessary element of that power—is once again demonstrated. So is the tactical interrelationship between the merchant marine and the navy. That ought to be enough. But there are, moreover, some apparently necessary reminders concerning inshore warfare, as a bonus.

However first a preliminary word about our story's two key players— Erich Raeder, the man who really built the *Kriegsmarine*, and Karl Dönitz, the one who took over from him and led that navy in its final days. Ships can be built; ordinarily they can be crewed and captained; but to command a fleet successfully—or, even more, a navy—requires talent, one that these two men provided—in plenty.

RAEDER (1876–1960)

Grossadmiral (Grand Admiral) Erich Raeder was a naval officer of the old school. Born April 24, 1876, he received his early education and training in the Kaiser's Imperial *Marine*. His father was a teacher and a secondary school principal. Raeder carried the values of this background with him throughout his career—rigidly.

Admiral Raeder was appointed Commander-in-Chief, Navy (ObdM) in October 1928, during the Weimar Republic's heyday. As Commander-in-Chief, Navy, he was unusual in that he had never commanded a ship at sea. He had spent much time at sea, however, as a junior officer and as chief of staff to von Hipper's battlecruiser squadron during World War I.

In fact, Admiral Raeder was professionally well-suited to his position as head of the Navy. As chief of staff to von Hipper he had shown a fine grasp of naval strategy, operations, and tactics. His book on cruiser warfare—published in the 1920s—was a standard work on the subject. Raeder also possessed the duller attributes of a good organizer, and he was a planner of considerable foresight. He supported the idea of a balanced navy. He kept a tight hold over every branch of the Navy, welding it into a hard, disciplined, capable organization. It was he who forged the instrument that his successor eventually used so well.

In foreign affairs Raeder's judgment was sure and matter-of-fact. He understood and developed the very sound principle of tying Germany's foreign policy to its naval strength. He realized that naval forces well used can make a foreign policy—especially a policy based on power. Until World War II, Raeder was able to argue this position.

Raeder's principal weakness was his mistaken belief that he had exceptional political sense and really understood German domestic politics. He had dabbled badly in the Reich's postwar political chaos, but his evident loyalty to the German Navy and his marked competence as a staff officer kept him in favor.

Raeder strictly enforced an order that his naval personnel were to take no part in politics. This professionalism effectively separated the Navy from the Nazi authorities. "Once burned, twice shy," perhaps.

Raeder—the grand seigneur—himself maintained a cautious, formal, reserved relationship with Hitler, establishing himself as a kind of father figure in naval matters, an area in which Hitler admitted to knowing little. Raeder adopted a sometimes hostile attitude toward other Nazi leaders, however, especially Goering. Hitler nevertheless respected Raeder, and promoted him to *Grossadmiral* in April 1939. Raeder remained Commander-in-Chief for a total of 15 years, until January 1943. In the end, the relationship turned sour and his professionalism cost him his job.

As his successor Raeder nominated a fellow surface-warfare officer, Rolf Carls. Hitler did not even accept this, Raeder's last recommendation, picking instead the highly successful Flag Officer, Submarines, Karl Dönitz, to replace him. Long after it mattered, however, Raeder's last point was made, as we shall see.

DÖNITZ (1891–1981)

Grossadmiral Karl Dönitz—professional submariner—commander of the *Kriegsmarine*, and in the last days head of state, carried of course the ultimate responsibility of this entire last chapter among German maritime enterprises. Admiral Dönitz's popular fame rests on his submarine warfare and on his momentary role as Hitler's successor. But in the long view of history, his main achievement will be seen as nothing else than as the architect of the greatest seaborne evacuation under fire ever carried out.

Karl Dönitz was born in 1891, in Grünau-bei-Berlin, a suburb of that great capital city. During World War I he saw service as an officer in the Imperial Navy, on famous light cruiser *Breslau* and in submarines. In the years after Versailles, he helped plan and organize Germany's forbidden submarine service. In 1935 Adolph Hitler gave him command of a now legitimized U-boat branch, as Commodore of Submarines.

Dönitz did not, during the prewar years, create a very strong public image. He remained in the background, concentrating on his U-boats, the development of which he promoted with exceptional skill. Himself a relatively young and ambitious officer, he identified with and won over the Navy's junior officers.

As the U-boat division grew, so did Dönitz. When World War II came, the submarines showed what they could do. Their "wolf pack" tactics were Dönitz's. He went from captain all the way to full admiral, but always in submarines. Along the way he became *"der Löwe"* (the Lion).

In January 1943 *Grossadmiral* Raeder fell out with Hitler over the question of Germany's further need for capital ships. As a result of a series of naval disasters, Hitler wanted to scrap all of them. Raeder resigned over the issue. Dönitz replaced him. Dönitz was 51, at the height of his powers.

Dönitz then quietly arranged to save most of the remaining big ships. They were hidden out of the way, most transferred to the Baltic's Fleet Training Squadron. Meanwhile, the *Kriegsmarine* concentrated on further expanding the submarine program.

Such is the skeleton of Dönitz's career, up to 1944. But more needs to be filled in for a better view of the man. His forebears were small farmers, pastors, officers, scholars. His father was an engineer, a member of Germany's new industrial middle class. In those days Berlin was the throbbing heart of the Prussian way of life; here the *volk* memories were to be seen on every side. He would have been expected to be worthy of those ideals, bearing himself as a Prussian officer. He did. He would save what he could.

Dönitz nonetheless had had little experience with the wider aspects of naval administration and strategy. While Raeder had been the strategist, Dönitz was the tactician. He would face many difficult problems—naval and national—in the coming days. There was some question even at the time about how well he would do. One such account will be considered here.

THE APPROACH

The purpose of this book, then, is to introduce the Anglo-American historian or naval history buff to yet another aspect of modern naval history not normally considered. (Another aspect was explored in my *The Cyrano Fleet: France and Its Navy 1940–42*, also published by Praeger.) Perhaps unavoidably, few of us in the normal course of things have much contact with or interest in the history of a former enemy. Differences in language only add an additional impediment. Nonetheless, the subject, once opened up, proves an entirely fascinating one.

Not covered here are the U-boat war, the surface raiders, the seizure of Norway, or the battle to cut the Russian convoys. Neither are the Battle of the Atlantic or that for the Mediterranean. These have all been covered adequately elsewhere. Most of us are already acquainted with these aspects of the war.

In light of the stated purpose, a sometimes difficult, even in this case perhaps impossible, series of choices had to be made concerning the proper tone of the work. Since one of the writer's first tasks is always to attract a readership among the broadest possible public, the detailed trappings of scholarship have again been left out. German naval terms have sometimes been translated with an eye to relating them better to U.S. experience.

This is not as easy a task as it sounds. The German "pocket battle-ships" were originally known to them as armored ships (*Panzerschiffe*). During the war they were retyped as heavy cruisers (*Schwere Kreuzer*). Compared to those of the U.S. Navy these ships, with their 11-inch guns, are probably best described as armored cruisers. Our heavy cruisers were limited to 8-inch guns. I call them armored cruisers.

Details have sometimes been arbitrarily generalized, in the interest of a smoother narrative. In exchange, a carefully selected bibliography has been included at the end.

A good portion of the material contained herein had to be gleaned, however, from books that dealt with the Baltic only in passing. A number of inevitable gaps had to be filled in by inference and analogy. Both English and German language sources had to be used. In light of the intended primary audience for this book, the bibliography includes as many English language references as I could find. German language sources have been somewhat more rigorously screened, but the key ones are there.

As can be seen, secondary sources have been utilized almost entirely, throughout. Much exhaustive work has already been done on the *Kriegsmarine* in Germany. I found more material than I actually needed, in the end. The principal problem was to maintain a certain level of detail, and then to integrate it all.

THE NUMBERS

On the other hand, very few of these sources agreed with each other on details. I realize that this is quite a common historical problem, but for several reasons, the difficulty was greater here. Up to now, most of the history has been written by naval officers, using limited sources or too fallible memories. Historians have only recently begun to exploit the German naval archives.

This problem becomes extremely acute with regard to evacuation statistics. Not everyone started counting at the same time and place (early, with the Finnish evacuation?). Not all those lifted out were listed on manifests, especially in the closing days. Not all manifests still exist. There must have been some double counting, as well, especially at transshipment ports. It is a wonder that valid numbers exist at all.

Taking the broadest view, merchant marine–based figures tend in general to be higher, Navy-based figures tend to be lower. As a rule, therefore, for naval matters Mallmann-Showell's book on the *Kriegsmarine* was, where possible, adopted as the final word. For matters which appeared to have been best handled by the merchant marine, authority was generally ceded to Schön's work. Where it seemed appropriate, I rounded everyone's statistics off to what appeared to me to be the nearest defendable number.

To give the reader some idea of the spread of evacuation statistics found between Navy-related sources and others, the following may be taken as typical:

Summary of *General von Steuben*'s passenger list as of 091130 February 1945, taken from Heinz Schön's *Ostsee '45:*

1600 wounded (bedridden)

1200 wounded (ambulatory)

 800 refugees

 100 special returnees (soldiers)

 270 naval medical personnel and other auxiliaries

  12 nurses taken aboard in Pillau

  64 antiaircraft personnel

  61 administrative personnel

 160 merchant marine personnel

4267 total

Figures taken from Mallman-Schowell's *Das Buch der Deutschen Kriegsmarine 1935–1945*:

3000 lost/300 saved, or 3300 total

Actually used by the author as best estimate:

3200 lost/300 saved, or 3500 total

There is little doubt in the author's mind, however, that much took place during the last days especially which was beyond accurate Navy record keeping and that, therefore, Schön's overall tally is the more nearly correct one.

The numbers can only, however, give us an idea of the orders of magnitude of the tasks. For that they are valid. The only sure number seems now to be that a total of well over 2 million people were in fact pulled out.

ORGANIZATION

A final word about organization of the book. A few additional liberties have been taken, naturally, in the interest of readability. Danzig (Gdansk) proper, Gotenhafen (Gdynia), Neufahrwasser, and Zopport (Sopot) are sometimes—especially later in the book—referred to simply as Danzig area, or even just Danzig. These places are all located within a few miles of each other, and are really part of the greater Danzig metropolitan area. Many atlases do not even identify anything other than Danzig. In any event, the names used throughout are the German ones.

It might be useful to note that the Appendixes include a short glossary of terms, names, and titles (German and English) scattered throughout the book and a list of the military abbreviations and acronyms used. These ought to be useful in their own right.

Many people and organizations helped with this book, one way or another. It could not have been completed without them. The Germans were especially helpful, particularly Professor Doctor Michael Salewski of the University of Kiel and Professor Doctor Peter Marquardt of Freiburg. The staff of the *Bundeswehr*'s military history research facility in Freiburg cheerfully helped a stray Yank. So did the archivist of the Naval School, Mürwick. That school's little museum even produced a number of original photographs for my use. Thanks, all! Needless to say, the errors are all mine.

The Trustees of the Imperial War Museum (London) kindly allowed access to their photographic files, and permitted reproduction of those pictures I chose. The library of the U.S. Naval Institute in Annapolis did the same.

It was *The Cruellest Night* (Dobson, Miller and Payne), picked up at London's Heathrow Airport during a layover, which introduced me to (and led me into) further study of the events recounted herein. Nothing I have found so far qualifies as the definitive history of what has to be one of the most enduring monuments to the human spirit in the face of great odds. Perhaps this book will generate such a work in the future. If so, good luck to whoever writes it. I would be among the first to welcome it.

1

Theater of Operations

THE DANISH STRAITS

Like the long, drawn-out politico-military agony about to be described here, the cold, far-off Baltic Sea is little known to most of us. The eastern and southern shores and the waters lapping them made up the stage upon which our story takes place. To better follow the events recounted and the kind of naval war with which the German Navy dealt, we need to know more about the Baltic and about constricted "narrow seas" in general than most readers do.

It would seem most understandable if we were to enter the Baltic as most did in those days, by sea. To do so, there is really only one way. From the North Sea east of Scotland, steam east. Enter the Danish Straits—the Skagerrak and the Kattegat. The wide mouth of the Skagerrak south of Norway rounds the Danish headland known as the Skaw and contracts into the Kattegat, running south. From there it soon narrows into a choice of three channels—from east to west, the Sound (the waters of which border both Denmark and Sweden) and the Great Belt and Little Belt (Denmark's). These three all lead into the Baltic proper at the Ostsee's far southwestern corner. That is where we enter.

The Danish Straits are international waterways. According to traditional international law, in peacetime the passage of warships is permitted. That includes submarines as long as they remain on the surface. Any attempt to transit the straits submerged (not a simple matter, in

1

The Baltic Sea (southern half including Danish Straits)

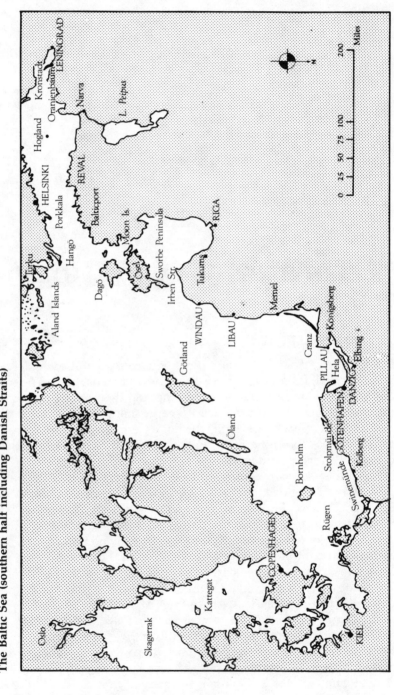

any case) can be met legally with protest, and if the protest is ignored, by force. Similarly, the laying of mines in these waters prior to the outbreak of war is illegal.*

The average depth in the Danish Straits is nowhere more than 15 fathoms, or 90 feet. Ground mines can be laid in most places, and moored mines in any area. Military geography favors Denmark; the straits are easily closed. Similarly, they are relatively easy to defend. Today's NATO must hope so.

There is a good short artificial route from the North Sea into the Baltic across the base of the Jutland Peninsula, usable by all but the largest ships, via Germany's Kaiser Wilhelm (North Baltic Sea, or Kiel) Canal. The *Kriegsmarine* was thereby enabled to transfer its forces from one sea to the other more or less at will.

THE OSTSEE PROPER

We are now in the Baltic proper, at its far southwestern corner. Ahead stretches the Ostsee, Northern Europe's inland sea. The Baltic itself runs generally north and south. It is seldom much more than 100 miles wide; in some places it is only half this figure. It extends 900 miles north from where we have just entered, past the Aland Islands, which close off the Gulf of Bothnia, to the gulf's northern tip.

The part of the Ostsee that concerns us most, say Danzig north to the Aland Islands, measures a distance of 360 miles. Another key distance— Danzig to Kiel—is 330 miles. From the mouth of the Sound to Danzig or Pillau is 260, to Libau, 300 miles. From the mouth of the Sound to the island of Bornholm measures an even 100.

The Baltic is a markedly and almost uniformly shallow sea. Its average depth is only 221 feet, or 37 fathoms. It is shallower in the northern parts, deeper in the southern. There are even scattered deeps, most off the steeper Swedish coast. With little fetch for large waves to use to build up, seas are short and steep. There is hardly any real tide. There are many islands, rocks, and shifting sand banks. Navigation can be difficult. Mines are very, very effective; mining is easy.

The whole Baltic region, lying as it does geographically so far north (54°N to 66°N) is one of long summer days and long winter nights. The weather is pleasant in the summer but very cold in the long winter. Storms are sudden and severe. In the winter, ice is everywhere, although

---

*In 1982 a U.N. Convention on Law of the Sea was finalized. In it, international straits are subject to a regime of transit passage (more liberal than innocent passage). Transit passage is nonsuspendable and allows both overflight and the submerged passage of submarines. The convention is not yet universal law. As an *historic* strait, these straits will be exempted, in any case.

south of the Alands icebreakers can easily and regularly keep channels and ports open. There is snow and fog.

The Baltic's eastern and southern coast is most characteristically low lying, sandy, thinly covered with pines as far as the eye can see. It is relatively featureless, lacking many good natural harbors.

The Baltic's eastern shore is broken primarily in two places: by the Gulf of Riga, and the Gulf of Finland. The latter is the most important. It averages only 30 miles in width, but it extends nearly 250 miles east, as far as Leningrad and Kronstadt, site of the Soviet Navy's principal Baltic base. The Finnish Gulf is regularly blocked by ice for three to four months of the year. The Gulf of Riga is dominated at its entrance by the Baltic islands—Dagö, Ösel, Moon, and others, off Estonia's western coast. The long, thin, Sworbe Peninsula, about which we shall soon hear, is an appendage of, and juts south from, Ösel. Riga Gulf also ices up in winter. The best eastern shore harbors lie here.

The Baltic's southern shore is somewhat more favored, being broken by the large Danzig Bay as well as several excellent if smaller harbors, including Swinemünde.

The German Navy's principal base was (and still is) located on the North Sea, at Wilhelmshaven, but it had long had major bases in the Baltic. Kiel was (and is) headquarters for the Ostsee. Kiel is only a small city at the Baltic's far southwest corner, at the inner (eastern) mouth of the Danish Straits, but it has a large naval base, extensive shipyards, and a fine port, all located along a ten-mile-long, deep fjord.

There was a base at Swinemünde. After 1939, there was another base at Danzig/Gotenhafen, nearer the action. There were others.

NARROW SEAS

Now, let us place the Baltic in its strategic and operational context. The Ostsee is strategically one of the world's "narrow seas." Conventional naval wisdom includes a number of empirical rules concerning operations in such waters. Theoretically applicable in 1939–1945, they were violated then (and are today) only at a fleet's extreme peril. Witness the British Royal Navy off Norway (1940).

Modern technology—especially that concerning air (and missile) power—has tended to deprive seapower of its ability to command narrow seas adjacent to enemy-held lands. Unless it enjoys overwhelming command of the sea, seapower can for any period of time dominate only waters distant from enemy naval and air bases.

Sea denial is sufficient for a land power when opposed by seapower. Sea control is always essential to a seapower.

In these waters, as a rule, a battle group sweeps in from over the horizon, asserts control within a determined area, and there does what it was sent to do. Its control will ordinarily only be the result of locally superior force, brought in by surprise. It may not last—or be expected to.

In these waters, to project power ashore, a fleet must include an air increment adequate for both defense and strike. Enemy air power properly handled can prevent blockades or other hostile exercises of seapower, close in.

Aircraft, small submarines, or even mines can achieve sea denial without requiring superior naval forces. Sea control requires, additionally, a substantial surface fleet. Witness the U.S. Navy in the Persian Gulf (1987–1988).

All waters within the narrow seas tend to take on at least some of the characteristics of inshore waters. The waters off every coast that are significantly affected by the land as well as the sea form a special theater of war. On these waters—offshore and inshore, both loosely called "inshore"—is fought a unique kind of naval war, often by peculiar-looking craft, indeed. Air power—today including missiles—plays a critical role here in both strategy and tactics.

The geographic extent of such waters cannot be rigidly defined. Extent depends on the power and operational range of all the lighter, cheaper weapons of naval warfare; mining and sweeping capabilities; range and capabilities of the shore-based aircraft involved.

The entire Baltic formed (and still forms) one of those theaters. Nowhere on its waters does the sea escape the influence of the land, nor does the land that of the sea.

Events in the Persian Gulf between 1980 and 1988 only validate and bring up to date all that we have just said. The Baltic and the Persian Gulf share most of the characteristics of such a special theater—although Gulf operations took place 40 years later and incorporated state-of-the-art weaponry, especially missiles.

There was really only one difference. While operations in that Gulf extended its whole length, they were at a considerably lower intensity level.

Here, the playboard is not just a flat featureless expanse of water. The character of these waters is intricate, governed by the nature of the coast, the nature and location of the natural traffic choke points (straits), the number and location of the harbors, and the depths. The weather and the sea themselves play big parts.

The coast is flat and featureless also, or it is not. There are islands, and/or sand banks, mud flats, rock pinnacles, leads, shoals, reefs. There are headlands, natural traffic choke points behind which lurked who knows what. There are straits, natural funnels through which all shipping must pass. The main shipping lanes are clearly marked and well known. They pass close to shore or they do not. Ports and harbors are many or few. They are icebound or killing hot. Deep water encourages submarine operation, shallow water really shallow mining. There are currents and tides. Too strong for mining? No problem? To the always sufficient natural hazards to navigation, in time of war, must be added those contributed by man. Air power will be a factor. Whose? Submarines will be a factor. Whose? In both cases, where and how? Ports can be covered by hostile artillery, or missiles, or not.

This is the *white water* and *brown water* (coastal and estuarine, as opposed to *blue water* or open ocean) navy's world. We in the United States knew it well in a simpler age, during the War Between the States. The tools to fight this kind of war are always left to others, now, or to be developed once the emergency arises.

INSHORE OPERATIONS

Operations in these waters involve large numbers of the smaller naval ships and craft—the *poussière navale* (naval dust)—to a degree initially not always realized by Mahanian (big ship, blue water) navies. In near waters like these, naval ships and craft have five real functions:

1. mine laying, offensive as well as defensive;
2. mine sweeping, keeping necessary sea lanes clear;
3. support of land operations (amphibious operations, gunfire support);
4. patrol of coastal waters;
5. escort of coastal convoys.

All of these five inshore operations assume in some measure a perhaps rudimentary but well practiced AA (antiaircraft) and ASW (antisubmarine warfare) capability. All are best carried out under protection of a closely cooperating naval air arm.

Given enough time, in these narrow waters, a land-based enemy can always concentrate all his available and perhaps overwhelming air (and missile) strength against any fixed target (a port) or any target that remains immobile in any one location too long (ships). Small craft with limited AA armament and ammunition capacity, and merchantmen, make the softest targets. But if the enemy is willing to pay the necessary price, any ship or craft within range is possible game. This includes AA cruisers, as we shall see.

Major combatants (aircraft carriers, battleships) may be too irreplaceable to be risked this close in, at least not for any considerable period of time.

Like it or not, however, no ship or craft can always keep entirely away, be she friend or enemy. All friendly ships and craft entering or exiting ports must cross this potentially very dangerous area.

The incidence of shipping is naturally greatest near the principal ports and straits. These can both be closed off at least temporarily by mines. They can be defended by mines and nets—and by aircraft, artillery, and missiles. Any enemy will lie in wait primarily off these ports, and off coastal promontories or headlands.

On narrow seas, direct air attack of ships in the dark being difficult, night passages of merchant traffic, close to shore, are usually feasible. Daytime passage under local air (fighter) cover is ordinarily possible; lacking that, daytime refuge in defended ports behind mines and nets must be the rule. Offshore mine barriers can add to the safety of transitting coastal traffic.

Offensively, mines can be carried to the enemy—to sink or damage his ships, of course. But they can be equally valuable simply disrupting his shipping; closing his ports, port approaches, and sealanes; and forcing him into a major minesweeping effort.

In every navy, the officers and men who man the inshore ships and craft tend to be a breed apart. Often they are reservists or hostilities-only types. In a different, earlier age they would be buccaneers or privateers. Emphasis here is placed, first, upon personal leadership. Then come practical pilotage and dead reckoning, seamanship, and ship-handling skill. A thirst for action does not hurt, either. Gunnery, communications, and engineering are relatively simple and direct.

Sea-related activities ashore have an immediate impact on events. Coastal surveillance and base defense are fundamental to control of these waters. Bases here are very likely to be advanced bases temporarily held, possibly nothing more than an anchorage and a pushed-forward tender. Under conditions of lesser intensity, even such things as anchored barges or (as we know) oil and gas exploration or production platforms become bases.

PEOPLES, NATION-STATES, AND NAVIES

No description of the Baltic theater would be complete without some mention of the peoples who border this sea. Operations on no narrow sea take place in a social vacuum. That the human geography of this area forms a critical piece of this operational mosaic will soon be amply demonstrated.

In brief, and cutting a few corners, the peoples who lived along the Baltic's eastern and southern shore are, from north to south and west, Finns, Estonians, Letts, Lithuanians, and Germans. This basic ethnic sequence is paralleled by a political one: Finland, Estonia, Latvia, Lithuania, and Germany (Memel, East Prussia, Danzig, West Prussia, Pomerania, and Mecklenburg, at the time). Historically, there has also been a Livonia (including pieces of eastern Estonia and Latvia, facing on the Gulf of Riga), and a Courland (coastal Latvia). By convenient extension, the whole of the Baltic's eastern shore, to include Estonia, Latvia, and Lithuania, has been known as Courland (Kurland in German). They will be so identified here from now on.

The whole of Courland was sprinkled with ethnic "Balt" Germans. In the thirteenth century, the Teutonic Knights and the Livonian Brothers of the Sword conquered the region later comprising Estonia and Latvia. The Teutonic Knights lost all but East Prussia in the fifteenth century, but descendants became the Baltic barons, holding large lands. The barons were gradually reinforced by invited landholders and by increasing numbers of bourgeois traders, settling in the towns and cities. These Germans never surrendered their separate identities. They had come to Christianize, and remained as a dominating elite. Hitler's Reich had begun conscious Germanization of the area, adding displaced nationals from elsewhere.

Before World War I, the Tsar's Imperial Russia dominated the eastern Baltic politically, holding Finland and the Baltic provinces, and part of Poland to the south. Having just been severely defeated in the Far East and having to rebuild its navy, it had abandoned Libau as its main Baltic naval base. The Baltic Fleet was recentered on the dockyard at St. Petersburg, the fortress of Kronstadt, and bases at Reval and Helsinki. This reflected a fundamental Russian strategy that committed the Baltic fleet to protection of the approaches to the capital and to defense of the Gulf of Finland, if nothing else. We shall see this again.

WORLD WAR I

German and Russian navies had faced off in the Baltic before. In 1914 both maintained considerable naval forces there, one basing at Kiel and elsewhere, the other at Kronstadt. The Kaiser generally stationed only his older battleships (pre-dreadnoughts) in the Baltic, although he could easily reinforce them at will from the North Sea via his new Kiel Canal.

Although there was normally a rough balance between the two Baltic fleets, when war came the Tsar hesitated to force a naval issue, thereby ceding effective control to Kiel. When the August guns opened up, the Germans sent out their U-boats and laid mines, the Russians (under outstanding Admiral von Essen, until his death) laid mines.

For Germany, keeping the Baltic shipping lanes open was vital. Germany—then as later—received most of its iron ore from Sweden via Lulea, a far northern port. Most of the grain from its eastern provinces and coal from the Ruhr was distributed by ship. During the fighting, the German Kurland armies had to be kept supplied and the long Baltic coast secured from the sea. The lanes were kept open; the armies were supplied; the coast was secured.

During 1915–1916, as the German armies moved into Kurland, there were the usual number of skirmishes—minor ones—at sea, and the Kaiser's Navy broke into the Gulf of Riga. This last had little effect, since the German Army failed to follow up the advantage gained. The German Navy suffered losses, but their domination of the Baltic was not ever seriously at risk. Submarines patrolled, mines were laid and swept. The merchantmen continued on their way.

In 1917 a large German amphibious operation was mounted to take the Baltic islands (Dagö, Ösel, Moon, and others). Defending Russian ships fought well but without luck. Russian battleship *Slava* (14,000 tons, built in 1905) was seriously damaged by German gunfire and had to be blown up by her crew. Destroyer *Grom* (1260 tons) was given up. The Germans, on the other hand, lost a number of smaller vessels to mines. The Germans occupied the islands.

Otherwise, as the Russian October revolution broke out, the maritime aspects of World War I to all intents and purposes drifted to an end—in the Baltic, at least. The Russian fleet withdrew into Fortress Kronstadt, where it rotted. Although the now dominant Germans held on at sea for another year, with the naval war at an end and revolution in the wind, they too finally fell apart.

THE INTERWAR PERIOD

It was sea power—British sea power—local national forces, and German land power which in 1918–20 at the close of World War I between them maintained order in the eastern Baltic. Finland as well as Kurland's new Estonia, Latvia, and Lithuania were working desperately to establish governments and at the same time fend off advancing Red armies. The Russians were naturally intent on recovering the former Imperial Russian provinces. In this they then failed. The British on the other hand had to apply considerable pressure before the German troops could be induced to leave for home.

In 1939 and 1940, Germany, on paper at least a temporary Russian ally, and with Britain neutralized, the Soviets did finally manage to re-occupy Estonia, Latvia, and Lithuania. Finland was forced to give up considerable border territory but retained its independence, after a short, vicious little war. Memel had been seized by the Reich earlier that year.

Historically, Germany had always looked to the east for room in which to expand its *Lebensraum* (living space), from the time of the Knights. As the USSR grew in power and resumed its version of Peter the Great's march toward the west, the Reich—no matter who governed in Berlin—could not but have felt uneasy about it. Kurland, therefore, was seized again in 1941 by *Wehrmacht* troops advancing on Red Leningrad, as Hitler turned on Stalin.

Finland in 1941—long in Berlin's political debt and now desirous of recovering territory lost to the Soviets in 1939—provided a ready-made German ally in the Baltic. Helsinki did join in, but it, too, had to be supported with troops and arms. The Finns fought well, but were just too few. They were to be forced out of the war, making a difficult separate peace in September 1944.

The Kurland political problem, then, was always a three-sided one—the Germans (Balts) versus the indigenous locals versus the Russians.

However, as in 1941, the *Wehrmacht* moved up, while the clumsy, repressive Soviet occupation had already begun experiencing local armed resistance. Germany was presented here with a rare opportunity for political gain. A cooperative confederation with the indigenous population should have been possible. The Nazis, however, intended only the eventual full incorporation of the Baltic states into the Reich. This was to be accomplished through Germanization, colonization, and resettlement of undesirable elements. German grenadiers were not to have shed their blood for nothing. Field Marshal Ludendorff's 1918 *Ostpolitik* was about to pay off.

Hitler therefore organized and imposed *Reichskommissariat Ostland*—90,425 square miles in all—including Estonia (roughly 1 million people), Latvia (1.8 million), and Lithuania (2.8 million), as well as a piece of western Russia. A large civil administration was duly installed. The *Reichskommissariat* by 1944 directly employed 2,235 Germans. There were between 10 and 12 thousand assorted occupation officials in Riga alone, the bulk of them performing economic and logistical tasks.

Now Balts simultaneously reassumed the role of governing elite with the backing of the SS. When in 1944 the *Wehrmacht* was forced back and out, however, there was no safety for them at all. Every man's hand was now against them, and flight was all that was left.

In the later stages of the German retreat, yet other issues arose. Lübeck and Danzig had been important Hansa cities; it was from these ports that the Germans traded into the Baltic. Danzig was separated from East Prussia in the Versailles peace, becoming a "Free City," to furnish Poland with a Baltic Port. Poland had also been furnished a corridor to Danzig and the sea, carved out of West Prussia, isolating East Prussia by land. This unnatural corridor was a *casus belli* in 1939, and so along with the Free City of Danzig, disappeared at once. But they had both acquired status as "stolen" Polish lands.

Moscow and Berlin had in 1939 effectively arranged the fourth partition of Poland, nothing less. In 1941 Berlin got it all. But as in 1944 the Russians advanced back westward, and kept coming, the Poles rose against both sides. Their rising proved futile, but again German settlers added to the stream of refugees fleeing west. Most were to come north to the coast sooner or later.

THE ULTIMATE STAKES

During World War II, at the height of its dark, evil power, Hitler's Reich dominated the Baltic. It had occupied Denmark (and Norway); Sweden was benevolently neutral; Finland was an ally. Poland was gone. German armies again marched in the footsteps and in the shadow of the Teutonic Knights, holding Kurland and investing Peter's "Window on the West," now Leningrad, confining the Russians there. Kurland was firmly under German control—secured by the *Wehrmacht*, populated with a large minority of Germanic settlers—the Balts—despite the continued efforts of both tsars and commissars. Balts, however, were still regarded as outsiders in a hostile land. An obvious asset to a victorious *Wehrmacht*, they would be a liability to a losing one.

This then is the arena in which our story is played out. Denmark held the door to the Baltic, through geography. But Germany held the key, being the paramount naval as well as military power, able to shift its ships from the North Sea to the Baltic via the Kiel Canal, at will. More on this as we go. Continental-minded Germany was about to get a lesson in sea power—a gut lesson, one close to home, that is.

For a whole host of historical and geopolitical reasons, the Germans had never been sea-minded. Until the Kaiser, that is, and then building a high seas fleet had only led to war. For a dedicated few, however, Scapa Flow was not the end. The Navy was reconstituted, and painfully rebuilt. Caught still unprepared by World War II, it was soon forced back on unrestricted submarine warfare. Even then, with never enough soon enough, it never fulfilled its role commanding the sea—except in the Baltic, that is.

Now the war was coming home—home to Germans. The Soviet army steamroller could not be stopped by the Navy, true. But the German Navy would rise to unimagined heights of organization and valor in rescuing what could be rescued by sea in the time it had. It had found a role worthy of it. For a while at least, in the Baltic it commanded the sea. It denied the sea to the Red Fleet, and itself exercised sea control almost wherever and whenever it needed to.

But the principal stake was the future of the German People trapped in the east.

2

The First Four Years

WEHRMACHT COMMAND STRUCTURE

World War II was fought by Germany, theoretically at least, with a unified armed force—the *Wehrmacht*. At no time during World War I had Berlin succeeded in achieving either a unified or even just a coordinated joint grand strategy. This had been a costly omission, and Berlin knew it. The Germans had very carefully studied the causes of their 1918 defeat. They meant to correct them.

In 1935, when Hitler renounced the Versailles Peace Treaty, a joint overall *Wehrmacht* headquarters (*Oberkommando der Wehrmacht* [OKW]) was set up. OKW was a rooftop body, meant to be a real joint directing, coordinating, inspecting, and advisory staff, superior to the three services (Army, Navy, and Air Force).

OKW was never allowed to mature. Hitler, already chief of state and political leader, had soon taken to himself the position of Supreme Commander of the Armed Forces. OKW rapidly developed into little more than the well-known *Führerhauptquartier* (Führer Headquarters). Hitler there gathered into his hands control over all aspects of German life as well as the war. The OKW staff could not long defend itself against Hitler's intuition and energy.

During most of World War II OKW thus never did much more than draft operation orders giving effect to the Führer's decisions. The Navy was represented on OKW only by a token few staff officers, too few to have any material input. The Army and the Air Force dominated OKW.

Subordinate to OKW were the three armed services, each now under its own commander in chief. Under this set up, the *Kriegsmarine* was separated from the Army and given a headquarters of its own—technically, *Oberkommando der Marine* (OKM)—coequal with the other two.

The *Wehrmacht* organization at first worked well enough as a planning unit. But in the later course of the war Hitler's OKW started to exercise direct control over specific operations in individual theaters of war. In proportion as it did this, it neglected its proper functions of general direction, inspection, and compromise. For this they duly paid.

The three service commanders in chief more or less directed their own operations within the framework laid down by OKW. Each chief had the right of direct access to Hitler. They periodically discussed future plans and current efforts with him. But seldom together. These "Führer conferences" were essentially reports of a chief to Hitler. Of true joint planning there was less and less, until there was none.

Towards the end, the influence of both Hitler and his OKW dissolved into a series of disconnected and isolated tactical moves. More and more, many of these had little bearing on or related to the actual state of affairs. At the end, each service went its own way. Hitler's eventual suicide (1945) merely confirmed the leadership situation that had already taken place.

PHASES OF THE WAR

In the Baltic, World War II was overall a bloody, inhuman affair. In humanistic terms, many aspects of what happened hardly make sense. But militarily, it divides itself into four distinct strategic phases. Since such a breakdown helps materially in understanding and in following the details of our story, it is here set out.

In military terms, the first phase of the war was marked by the German (re-)conquest of Poland and the readmission of Danzig to the Reich, the partition of Poland, and the USSR's seizure of the three eastern Baltic states. This initial phase lasted from September 1939 until June 1941, although only the first month saw any actual fighting—by the Germans anyway.

The second phase (June 1941 to December 1941) is taken up by the German (and Finnish) advance and occupation of the eastern Baltic coast and most of the Gulf of Finland. This was almost a German triumphal parade, although Leningrad, Kronstadt, and Oranienburg were never taken, either then or later. The Baltic became virtually a German lake.

The Baltic war's third phase was a period of strategic stalemate. This halcyon time lasted from January 1942 until January 1944. For the *Kriegs-marine*, this stalemate was maintained until March or even for some aspects until mid-September 1944, well more than two and a half years.

The fourth and last phase of the war (January 1944 until the end in May 1945) was marked by the German retreat—soon a flight—back across the Ostsee into the homeland, and then still further back through its eastern marches to the west.

It is this last phase that we have chosen to emphasize most here. It was during this period that Germany's maritime services—led by the *Kriegsmarine*—achieved their real place in history. It is the kind of place allowed but few. The Baltic could be a cruel sea. It was a cruel war. But a people was saved.

WORLD WAR II BEGINS

For the *Kriegsmarine*, it was in the Baltic itself that World War II began—at Danzig. The Navy touched it off with the deliberate shelling of the Polish fort on the Westerplatte, in the Vistula River estuary, dominating Danzig. Old battleship *Schleswig-Holstein* bombarded and the 225-man naval assault group "Hennigsen" landed to seize it on September 1, 1939. Westerplatte fell a week later.

At this point, the Polish Navy (Rear Admiral Unrug) counted as available a destroyer, a minelayer, five small submarines (the submarines all escaped to either Allied or neutral ports, later), two old torpedo boats, two gunboats, six small minesweepers, and auxiliaries. It was only a token force; three destroyers had been sailed to Britain before hostilities began. There was also a minelayer, about which more later.

The Polish Navy was rapidly overwhelmed by superior and ready German naval forces (Generaladmiral Albrecht): old battleships *Schleswig-Holstein* and her sister, *Schlesien;* light cruisers *Nürnberg, Leipzig,* and *Köln;* nine destroyers; an S-boat flotilla (S-boats were *Schnellboote,* German motor torpedo boats; they were known to the Western Allies as E-boats); a minesweeping flotilla; and other supporting units. There was *Luftwaffe* support.

The naval contest was soon over. The Polish surface ships (never a large threat) were finally put out of action in harbor by German aircraft, one by one. The Polish minelayer laid her mines with their firing mechanism still set on safe. When on September 3, Britain and France declared war on Germany, the *Kriegsmarine*'s modern cruisers and destroyers could safely be sent to the North Sea to face them. However, Admiral Unrug and 4000 men stubbornly held out on the flat, sandy Hela peninsula for another month, surrendering only on October first.

THE BALTIC RED BANNER FLEET—1941-1944

In June 1941, when Hitler turned on Stalin, the Soviet Red Banner Baltic Fleet (Baltflot, Vice Admiral Tribuc) was one of Russia's two major fleets. On paper it constituted a formidable force. It boasted two 23,300-ton old battleships, modernized post-dreadnoughts launched in 1911. They mounted 12, 12-inch guns each, and were still dangerous when met. They would have been more than a match for the two much older German battleships regularly stationed in the Baltic.

Baltflot also included two heavy cruisers, each of them displacing 8000 tons and mounting nine 7.1-inch guns (the *Kriegsmarine* normally kept none in the Baltic at all). In addition, there were two large destroyer leaders (2900 tons, carrying five 5.1-inch guns), 12 new destroyers, seven old destroyers, and seven torpedo boats. There were 65 submarines of various types, considered a major threat. There were six minelayers and 33 minesweepers, another important threat. There were a reported 48 motor torpedo boats. These were all backed by the usual auxiliaries and service craft.

Baltflot controlled its own integral naval air arm, equipped at this point with some 600 planes. This gave it an organizational advantage the *Kriegsmarine* was seldom able to match.

Baltflot's main base was located at Kronstadt, on Kotlin Island, in the approaches to Leningrad proper. It maintained forward bases at Reval, at Windau, and at Libau. There was also one at Hangö, taken from the Finns the previous year. This reflected the historic basing pattern. Obviously, geography had not changed since the days of the tsar.

The Soviet fleet—like all the others—suffered in 1941 from several fundamental disabilities, all affecting its operational readiness. In the Stalin purges of the 1930s, its officer corps had been decimated. Its rulers did not really understand seapower, anyway. Initiative and flexibility were markedly lacking, orders being detailed to the extreme. Its leaders feared making mistakes, or even to be seen as having been wrong. On the other hand, its gunnery was good, and it would fight if cornered, as it always had.

Baltflot was unquestionably at least the short-run dominant Baltic fleet, numerically capable of denying free use of the sea to any enemy. If it had challenged the Germans with its full strength, it could have materially affected Baltic operations. But it was considered only as the seaward extension of the Red Army, and the Red Army was falling apart. Its big ships remained in port.

Under strict orders not to initiate hostilities itself, in 1941 Baltflot was slow to react. When it did, Baltflot responded with extensive tactical mining, and by establishing a host of additional small bases on various islands for its submarines and torpedo cutters (motor torpedo boats). It also laid its own minefields across the entrance to the Finnish Gulf. But that is all it did.

THE *KRIEGSMARINE*—1941–1944

In 1941, when the war with the USSR began, the *Kriegsmarine*, besides defending the German-held coast, was to prevent any attempt by Baltflot to break out of the Baltic, and as soon as it could, destroy it. As the capture of Leningrad would eliminate Baltflot's both principal and last Baltic base, and so force the issue, there were to be no major secondary operations before then. Pure Mahan, this was. First, gain command of the sea. Too pure.

Once Baltflot had been eliminated, the *Kriegsmarine* was to then ensure the full resumption of Baltic shipping. This last would involve mine clearance along shipping lanes, perhaps convoy, and escort. Command having been gained was to be used.

Although overall much stronger, the German Navy was having to fight on a number of fronts. The most they could at this point spare for the Baltic were ten minelayers, about 70 minesweepers of different types, and two tenders carrying motor pinnaces for sweeping in shallow water. There were two old battleships and five submarines (U-boats) from the training squadron, and 28 motor torpedo boats (S-boats). The *Kriegsmarine* had no naval air arm of its own, and was forced to rely on the general air force for support.

There was also a Finnish Navy with two coast defense ships, 3900 tons each, six motor torpedo boats, five submarines, along with assorted minesweepers and patrol craft. They materially assisted in the Gulf.

In 1941 German Baltic naval plans were strategically defensive, conceived more or less autonomously and executed the same way. No substantive naval support for land operations was laid on. None was requested. (To this there was one exception. Libau was captured by the Army, but with the assistance of naval assault detachment "von Diest." Commander von Diest was killed in the action.)

Initially the Army looked to the Navy only for logistic support, and planned for little of that. The Army's speed of advance, as well as the inadequate road net and a shortage of transport, gradually forced it to change, drawing more and more on the Navy's strategic lift.

If the *Kriegsmarine*'s Baltic war plans were strategically defensive, tactically they were not. German S-boats began to lay the new magnetic mines off key Soviet ports almost at once. With the Finns cooperating, more mines were laid in the entrance to the Finnish Gulf. This left the Soviets with the choice of either holding up their shipping until the entrances were swept, or, as at Hangö, running the ships through anyway and taking the inevitable losses. Apparently, they did both. In

September and October, the Baltic islands were cleared by troops ferried across from the nearby mainland in a makeshift lift. Support was provided by light cruisers *Leipzig, Emden,* and *Köln.* With this went the myriad small Soviet bases sprinkled throughout the area.

BARBAROSSA IN THE BALTIC

As the *Wehrmacht* swiftly cleared the Baltic states, it forced Baltflot to abandon its newly acquired and still incomplete bases at first Libau, then Windau, and finally Reval. Soviet submarines suffered heavy losses in the German minefields, and from German U-boats and S-boats. Several of the larger Soviet ships suffered serious damage from the air. Those ships which could not be brought back were scuttled. The shore facilities were blown up.

By October, a main concern of Baltflot became the evacuation of its large base at Hangö. The pullout—if there was to be one—had to be completed before the beginning of the ice season in December. Four large and a number of small convoys carried it out between the last of October and the first of December, at great cost. Three destroyers and at least ten other ships were sunk in its course. With never enough time to properly clear passages through minefields, most were lost to mines.

On December 3, during the last convoy out, transport *Josef Stalin* (7500 GRT) struck several mines. She was loaded with both troops and ammunition, and the munitions blew up. Four thousand of the troops were killed. Many were taken off by the escorts. Left dead in the water, the wreck drifted on until she was found and beached by German patrols. On board they discovered 2000 more men still alive.

The 65 available Soviet submarines accomplished little. As early as July 12, German commercial as well as military supply shipping had been resumed. Soon it often proved possible to proceed without escort, although large ships with valuable cargoes (troops, ammunition) were never sailed alone. By the close of 1941, 27 Soviet submarines had been lost. Soviet submarines just did not seem to be able to function to exploit their admittedly widespread targets.

By the time the ice set in, closing the Gulf of Finland, the Red fleet had withdrawn to its main base at Kronstadt. From then until it broke out again three years later, there it stayed. It trained; it attacked the German and Finnish ships laying and reseeding the minefields helping keep them in. Its guns supported the Leningrad front and the Oranienbaum pocket. It continued to feed a trickle of submarines into the Gulf.

Meanwhile, the theoretically weaker German forces had been easily able to lay thicker and more extensive minefields (defensive ones, now) off Libau, Windau, the Irben Strait north of Dagö, and between Nargön and Porkkala. The waters north of Juminda (Estonia) was heavily mined to protect Reval, the major port just to the west.

INTERREGNUM IN THE BALTIC

Thus by 1942 Germany was supreme in the Baltic. This large inland sea was effectively a German lake. During the next two years, the *Kriegs-marine* there carried out an assortment of low intensity but important tasks: continuing to keep the Soviet Baltic fleet penned up, ready to destroy it if ever it attempted to break out; supporting Finland in the war; and keeping a friendly but alert eye on benevolently neutral Sweden. It was further to perform the by now routine defense of the German coast against landings and raids by hostile forces; to protect the heavy and critical coastal shipping; to support the Army in Kurland; and to train. Since it enjoyed as complete a command of the Baltic as anyone could, it did all these things.

Sweden possessed a well manned small fleet, one which theoretically could do a lot of damage in a surprise attack. But any threat of Sweden entering the war on the side of the Allies had to be a remote one at this point. Swedish ties to Germany and Finland were strong. Nonetheless, a properly prudent Reich had always to be prepared for the worst. An even token, patently reinforceable, fleet was a continuing reminder of its interest and reach.

The Baltic was ideal as a training area for the Navy. It was at this point protected from any serious interference by the Allies. It was far from Allied air bases. It was quite big enough and both shallow and deep enough, in places, to allow the most rigorous U-boat work-up. It was handy, for all types of ships. There was a Fleet Training Squadron— and two U-boat training divisions, and numerous small craft training flotillas. And Sweden to visit.

Denmark also had a well manned, if tiny, fleet. Until 1943, under the 1940 occupation agreement, the Danish fleet remained intact under Danish command, concentrated as a unit at Copenhagen. As the Nazi war effort began to show signs of strain, the Danish fleet surfaced as a somewhat more potential risk. Yet Danish ties to Sweden were also close. There were limits on what action could be taken. In 1943, under German pressure, the little fleet was dispersed to some 18 scattered anchorages. Its important elements remained at short notice for steam, however. The impasse was only resolved when the tiny fleet scuttled itself, avoiding seizure.

In 1943, also, the many separate minefields laid by the *Kriegsmarine* at the entrance to and inside the Finnish Gulf became the basis for an ambitious German overall mine plan. If Baltflot could not be destroyed, it could really be kept locked in. During the previous year (1942) the various fields had been connected to make three continuous lines of mines stretching all the way across the Gulf. These were maintained and defended. When these did not succeed in wholly preventing the passage of Soviet submarines, the German Navy reinforced the middle line with a string of nets. Effectiveness from then on was total.

THE TIDE BEGINS TO TURN

During the spring, summer, and fall of 1944, as German defeats on other fronts began to affect the *Wehrmacht's* position in the Baltic area itself, the high water of Nazi conquest there also slacked off. The tide ebbed almost imperceptibly at first, then with steadily increasing rapidity. As the German position crumpled, the Navy was offered the greatest role it had ever had in all its history. Practically by itself, it was to rescue the Germans of the eastern Baltic.

Steel ships, iron crosses, and refugees highlighted a tumultuous, tremendous enterprise critical to a major segment of the German *Volk*. Just as a still shining episode in the triumph of brave men over great odds, the naval story is one well worth telling, again and again.

In January 1944 the massive Soviet counterattacks back westward had finally reached the Baltic area. The first Soviet advance occurred here when the German front was pushed back from Leningrad and Oranienbaum to Narva and Lake Peipus. Naval operations were for the breakout organized around three Baltflot battle groups: one built around damaged and grounded old battleship *Petropavlovsk* and including two destroyers and a gunboat; another centered on old battleship *October Revolution*, three cruisers (*Tallin*, *Maxim Gorky*, and *Kirov*), and two destroyers; and a third smaller one which included four destroyers and three gunboats. Their organization threatened greater things.

Grossadmiral Dönitz at this period still supported—was particularly interested in, even—all-out defense of the whole Baltic area, including maintenance of the Kurland beachhead, as he needed time to build and train crews for his new generation of submarines. The new Types XXI and XXIII could still bring the Reich victory. They would have to work up in the Baltic.

The *Kriegsmarine* battened the hatches down for heavy weather. It was at first affected little, however. German laying and maintenance of mines and nets continued much as before. For the moment, the inner part of the Gulf of Finland remained sealed off.

German land forces around Lake Peipus working to stabilize a front (Narva–Lake Peipus Line) with scanty forces were supported in this by a flotilla of ferry-barges and S-boats. When the position was outflanked from the south, the front crumpled and the German retreat resumed.

The guerrilla war fought in the Gulf between the opposing light forces did then begin to pick up. Up to then, German mine and net barrier patrols had been composed of M-boats (minesweepers), R-boats (motor minesweepers), armed trawlers, drifters, and naval gun barges. Now, however, it became necessary to bring up destroyers, torpedo boats, and S-boats.

Massed attacks by enemy motor torpedo boats on German forces, fiercely fought at close quarters, began to yield Baltflot occasional successes. T–31 and M–37 were sunk by skillfully handled enemy boats, the *Kriegsmarine* thereby losing a valued torpedo boat and a minesweeper in June.

As the Gulf littoral was cleared, and advanced coastal airfields were captured, intervention by Soviet aircraft in the Gulf's surface affairs did slowly pick up, also. (The German barrier patrols were first strongly attacked from the air on March ninth.) By now the Red Air Force had been so strengthened that German patrols in the minefields and in Narva Bay had to take refuge at their bases during daylight hours.

In an attempt to provide the Gulf patrols with support, AA cruiser *Niobe* (former Dutch 3500-ton cruiser *Gelderland* now carrying eight heavy 105-mm [4.1-inch] AA guns as well as many smaller ones) was sent into the Finnish leads early in July. But even she was lost on July 16, when she was attacked by some 130 enemy bombers, torpedo planes, and fighters.

During July then, in the face of all this stepped-up enemy activity, German minefield patrols did finally have to be abandoned. It was then only a matter of time before the mine and net barriers were either bypassed or paths were cleared through them. This was a defeat of tremendous proportions. Sooner or later, the Russians would appear in the Baltic proper.

HOGLAND—THE MARKER

High water for the German Navy in the Baltic first began to ebb visibly in mid-September 1944. This date is perhaps an arbitrary one. The operation in question was a minor one, even part of a military operation. But the operation opened with the Germans on the tactical attack and closed with them pulling back, having suffered a clear defeat. So, small-scale though it might have been, the Hochland/Hogland affair becomes a convenient naval and maritime marker, symbolizing larger events. The great evacuation by sea, under fire, had begun.

Uncharacteristically, this marker operation was wholly a military affair. There would be few like this again until the great lift drew to its end. Still, it will do.

To better set the stage, a little more background history is in order. When Hitler's Germany attacked the USSR in June 1941, Finland allied itself with Berlin, hoping thereby to regain territory lost to Moscow during a local 1939–1940 war. (Historically, the relationship between

Helsinki and Berlin has long been close. German troops played a significant role in winning Finland its independence after World War I.)
In spite of some initial Finno-German successes, in 1944 the Russians—
as part of their general advance to the west—pushed across the border
and threatened to overrun the land. By September Helsinki was forced
to sign an armistice. As part of the ceasefire, Finland was required to
ask its German allies to leave, and to grant naval, military, and air bases
to the Soviets. Those troops that could, duly left—41,420 of them—in
an administrative lift from Finland's southwestern ports.

When in September Finland was forced out of the war, and in spite
of the terms of the armistice, a *Kriegsmarine* task group attempted to
seize the small, strategically useful Finnish island of Hogland, in the
east central Gulf of Finland. Hogland under German control would help
keep Soviet naval forces bottled up at the far eastern end of the Gulf,
at Kronstadt. The Red Baltic Fleet had so far been immobilized behind
three different mine barrages, one of which was backed by an antisubmarine net stretching south from the Porkkala Peninsula to near Reval.
The easternmost line of mines was anchored on Hogland, in part.

On the day, a scratch force of minesweepers (M-boats), motor minesweepers (R-boats), and other light craft put troops ashore. But the
Finnish garrison resisted, and called for help from the Russians. The
Finns were well supported by Soviet aircraft and the attempt failed. The
German force had to withdraw, losing four landing craft, one R-boat,
and four smaller boats. One torpedo boat was also sunk by Soviet aircraft
while covering the withdrawal. This was a slow start, but it was the
beginning of the end, as far as our story goes. It was a bad omen of
things to come, as both the scale and pace of evacuation operations
escalated rapidly from here on.

Also in mid-September, Russian troops finally broke through to the
Gulf of Riga. Estonia was cut off and had to be hurriedly evacuated.
The last ships left Tallin on September 22. The last convoy left Reval
September 23: four steamers and a hospital ship escorted by four torpedo
boats of the 3rd Torpedo Boat Flotilla. The stream of heavy laden naval
and merchant vessels plodded south and southwest under continuous
Soviet air attack, but only one merchantman was sunk.

In October, Russian forces landed on the Baltic islands (Dagö, Ösel,
Moon, and others), offshore. They successfully seized all except the
Sworbe Peninsula, at the southern point of Ösel. The Peninsula held
out until November 22, thanks to naval gunfire support supplied by a
succession of ships: armored cruiser *Lützow*, destroyers, torpedo boats.
That night in difficult weather, landing craft escorted by M-boats and
R-boats managed to evacuate 4500 troops, losing only one barge. A
relatively minor operation, indeed, but a good drill.

BREMERHAVEN

Then at the end of October an incident occurred, the primary significance of which lay apart from the ship. Sad as it was, it dramatically demonstrated that all was not really well with the existing convoy and escort system. Steamer (transport) *Bremerhaven* (5356 GRT) departed Windau for Gotenhafen 291730 Oct with 3171 persons on board. These included 1515 wounded (1200 bedridden, 315 ambulatory), 680 assorted refugees, 511 Todt Organization workers, 200 SS, 156 female *Wehrmacht* auxiliaries, and 109 others including crew. Ninth Escort Division had provided two M-boats as escorts.

At 300930 *Bremerhaven* was attacked near Hela from the air and set afire. She sank the next day at 0730. Of those on board, a total of 410 was lost, but 2795 people are known to have been saved. Nonetheless, the rescue efforts could have done more.

The Navy had not shone during this incident. The largely informal, rather relaxed, and casual organizations and procedures developed in the halcyon days of 1942 and 1943 were evidently no longer adequate for the mounting fury of 1944. A searching postmortem was set under way.

Angry questions were raised widely in Navy circles. The convoy's routing was challenged (apparently, the inshore route south had become safer than that across the open sea). The disorganized procedures whereby information relating to the sinking was handled and routed by staff caused comment. So did equipment furnished the transports. So did convoy defense. So did coordination of the rescue effort. Ninth Escort Division first heard the news at 310930, a whole day later, and then it learned of the unfortunate loss only through overhearing a third-party radio conversation. Much needed to be straightened out, urgently.

Bremerhaven's loss led to two changes: a reorganization of naval escort services as well as the Baltic command structure; and the issuance of the first of a series of Standing Convoy instructions. Ninth Escort Division—obviously overextended, now that the fighting was heating up—was relieved of responsibility for the north German coast, and that was turned over to a newly created Tenth Division. A number of flag officers were assigned to other posts, or were retired.

Standing Convoy Instruction No. 1 initiated the process of designation of convoys, ports of departure, directions of sailing, and destinations. It carefully delineated who was in command, responsible for what, when. A convoy teletype net was set up. It was long overdue. We shall develop the final command structure further as we go.

At the same time, the Red Army smashed its way to the sea between Libau and Cranz, isolating Memel (evacuated in January). Their push north up along the coast toward Libau was frustrated by German gunfire support laid on by a small force of cruisers and destroyers, giving the German Kurland armies time to organize a defense which lasted right up to the end of the war. Unfortunately, this Kurland hedgehog—it included both Libau and Windau and contained over 500,000 men—now could only be sustained by sea. It added considerably and continually to the strain on Baltic lines of communication all during the rest of our story.

BALTFLOT

The Red Army's advance westward after lifting the siege of heroic Leningrad along the Gulf of Finland, followed by Finland's withdrawal from the war, the loss of Hogland, the loss of Estonia, and the rapid clearance of the Baltic islands finally made it possible for the Russians to break Baltflot out into the Baltic itself. They had employed their surface units to support these operations and to clear away the mine barrages and antisubmarine nets blocking the way. The route out was now open.

According to the records, Baltflot at this point had the following fully operational vessels: one battleship (the other had been damaged from the air), two heavy cruisers, two destroyer leaders, eight to ten destroyers, 20 submarines, 78 torpedo cutters, some 300 minesweepers of various sizes and types, and a miscellany of supporting craft. By the close of 1944, the fleet air arm numbered perhaps 700 planes.

The stage thus had indeed been set for what looked to be a hard time in the Baltic. If Baltflot ever did get loose and assume an active role, it would be able to drive the Germans from these waters. The Red Fleet had not fled to the protection of internment in Sweden; it seemed ready to fight.

The *Kriegsmarine* moved what little more it could still spare into the Baltic, and began laying even more mines. Then it waited.

Once Baltflot had accomplished all this, however, from here on to the end of the war—for six months more—not a single Soviet surface warship destroyer or larger vessel ever appeared in the Baltic proper.

Yet, German sea lines of communication (SLOCs) presented a vulnerable and worthwhile target. Slow and weakly escorted German convoys were always within reach. The Red Fleet nonetheless sank not one major enemy vessel—naval or merchant—by gunfire. From here on in, it employed only aircraft, submarines, and torpedo cutters, doing what damage it could with them. The Germans, then, were most vulnerable in their port approaches, and at their ports.

As could be expected—recognizing the Red Air Force's considerable expertise in tactical warfare—the first and biggest single Soviet success came in mid-December, when their aircraft carried out a two-day massed attack on Libau, key to the Kurland *Festung*, sinking four steamers and damaging eight others. However, this attack cost the Red Air Force some 100 planes. Once the antiaircraft defenses of the port were strengthened, further air attacks there achieved nothing.

As 1944 closed, maritime statistics presented a grim picture. From January to December—during the whole year—the Germans had lost 70 merchantmen, totalling 153,275 gross registered tons (GRT). But 53 of them, adding up to 122,276 GRT, were lost between September and December, that is, in the last four months. Projections on future losses could not have been good. Soviet bombs, mines, and torpedoes were taking a seriously increased toll.

EBB TIDE

In contrast to previous years, the winter of 1945 brought no real respite in operations at sea. In January, as a matter of fact, our story takes a quantum leap in intensity. Baltflot now controlled ice-free bases for its submarines and light surface craft. Advances on land steadily provided it with more of them, and with airfields. Baltflot made full use of them.

During the remaining months of World War II, the same sequence of events kept repeating itself. Inland the Red Army broke through thin German lines, cut off large areas, and blocked roads to the west. Evacuation over land was impossible. German military units retreated to the coast, accompanied by many thousands of civilians fleeing the Reds. The only road to safety was the sea. Ports had to be held, supported by the *Kriegsmarine*'s cruisers and destroyers' guns, until evacuation could be organized and completed. At the same time, the German Navy's smaller ships and craft escorted the convoys, incoming and outgoing. Baltflot did all it could to stop them.

On January 12, the Red Army opened its final offensive across the Vistula and into Germany proper. East Prussia was soon cut off. Its surviving defenders were compressed into bridgeheads in the Königsberg/Pillau and Elbing areas. By the last days of January, Pillau was packed with frightened refugees. Wounded filled the hospitals, troops filled the streets.

On January 26, an ammunition dump in the fort blew up, causing widespread damage. Hundreds were killed; on the night of the explosion alone an estimated 28,000 refugees had been added to those already there seeking transportation out by sea.

Steady bombing was turning the already damaged town into rubble. The stink of death and blood, plaster and fire, was everywhere. Still the refugees came, panic-stricken at the revenge being taken as the enemy pressed remorselessly west. So too came the ambulances loaded with men wounded in the great battles that marked the fighting retreats in the east—so, too, scattered groups of technicians, necessary still.

From here on in, ideology no longer mattered. Well-being could not be thought of. The war had become a basic question of stark survival, for individuals and for the nation. Desperate measures were called for. They were produced, in blood, by a great navy. What, exactly, was this navy?

3

The *Kriegsmarine*

THE REAL ISSUE

The events recounted here have significant implications for the entire German Navy for as long as it exists, a fact which it must already know. The German Navy—Imperial *Marine, Reichsmarine, Kriegsmarine,* or *Bundesmarine*—has had an unusually difficult time finding itself. First formed in 1848, perennially second-best, it twice had to face the mightiest sea-power in modern times (the Royal Navy) and had always lost.

The dominant German military organization—the Army—looked on the upstart Navy only as a coastal arm of itself, useful for little, if anything a waste of precious resources. It paid it scant attention, in any case. That situation was about to be corrected, hopefully for good.

In effect the personal creation of Kaiser Wilhelm II, the first ruler to see Germany as a world power with significant overseas economic and colonial interests to defend, the Imperial *Marine* (as we know it) burst on the international scene around the turn of the century. Inevitably, it ended up challenging Britain. This led to and probably helped cause, World War I (1914–1918). Germany's use of unrestricted submarine warfare (1917, the second time) brought in the United States against it and guaranteed it would lose the war. The fleet mutinied (1918). Surrendered and interned at Scapa Flow, it supposedly saved its honor by there scuttling itself (1919). (Some 200 U-boats were also surrendered as part of the price of armistice; like the 74 surface ships at Scapa Flow,

they were interned pending a final peace. It was the surface ships at
Scapa Flow which were scuttled by their crews. A few were shot doing
it.) The only great fleet action it had fought—Jutland (1916)—didn't
change a thing.

A further word concerning a naval event little known here that must
have been crucial to our story seems in order. In October 1918, despite
Jutland, the Imperial Navy remained a very powerful, virtually intact
surface as well as submarine force. The admirals had therefore determined on one last fleet effort finally to justify the fleet's existence, and
hopefully to strengthen Germany's bargaining position at the by then
inevitable peace talks. They could just conceivably have changed history
had they carried it all off.

According to the admirals' plan, German light cruisers were first to
lead destroyers on a series of raids in the Thames estuary on a scale
sufficient to draw the British Grand Fleet down from its Scottish bases.
Extensive minefields were to be laid across its path. Numbers of U-boats
were to lay in ambush for it. The High Seas Fleet was then to fall upon
an already severely hurt, badly disorganized Grand Fleet as it continued
south, at the most advantageous time and place. It was a bold plan, but
there was little to lose.

This quite rational move, pursued to the utmost, by severely damaging
the British fleet could indeed have greatly strengthened the relative
German negotiating position in the coming talks. The virtue of the plan
was that it did not really matter whether the Germans won or lost,
provided only that they did inflict severe damage on the enemy. On
paper, at least, this was a fairly safe bet. The Imperial *Marine* was at
least to earn its salt, and just when the Fatherland needed it most.

At the end of October, the High Seas Fleet actually did get under way
preparatory to setting the plan in motion, assembling in Schillig Roads.
So far, the British had no idea that anything untoward was going on.

At this point, the plan simply fell apart. The crews of the larger German ships—too many too long idle—were joined by the shore staffs in
what became a general mutiny. Morale had fallen too low, there was
too much war-weariness, there was on the lower decks no interest in
any death or glory ride. Red flags were hoisted, arms broken out.

This, the Imperial Navy's final effort to affect the war's outcome,
thereby died stillborn. Under these most ignominious conditions, can-
cellation was the only possible end. For the older officers and petty
officers, this all had taken place only 25 years—one war—ago. They
remembered it, grimly.

REICHSMARINE-KRIEGSMARINE

At the close of World War I (1919) the Second Reich (the hopeful
Weimar Republic), as much by reflex action probably as anything else,

re-established the Navy, calling it now the *Reichsmarine*. Vaguely, it was to help defend the Reich against Poland and France, and Russia. It would dominate the Baltic—hopefully.

In a typical Versailles compromise, satisfactory to no one, a German Navy had been allowed by the Peace Treaty, even though the authority was a severely restricted one. A Reich Naval Office was established (1919) to salvage what it could from the old navy, and to oversee the new one. The first concern of the *Reichsmarine* was to put into service those ships left to it, most of which were very old and in a poor state of repair—and, to dispose of the rest.

Under the Versailles Treaty, the Reich was allowed not more than six active armored ships, six cruisers, 12 destroyers, and 12 torpedo boats, manned by 15,000 full-time officers and men. Submarines were forbidden, as were aircraft. A small reserve of ships was permitted, but no officers or men. Limits on replacement construction were set out in very careful detail. Circumvention of the treaty began almost at once.

Beginning in 1920, the *Reichsmarine* managed slowly to bring into service a few antique light cruisers built around the turn of the century, some old but useful torpedo boats, and, finally, six veteran ships of the line, pre-dreadnoughts built between 1903 and 1908. Around this ambiguous core the new fleet was to be born.

By 1925, reorganization was completed and the first of the *Reichsmarine*'s new ships began to appear—durable light cruiser *Emden* (5600 tons, 29 knots) and 12 new torpedo boats (930 tons, 33 knots). Although quite good designs, however, these tended to be only continuations of World War I models. *Emden* still had single-gun turrets.

The first entirely new state-of-the-art ships came in the years 1926–1930, when the initial three of an eventual total of five 6650-ton light cruisers joined the fleet. These were the first German ships to have director control of the guns, the 5.9-inch guns being placed in triple 5.9-inch turrets. Both were forbidden by Versailles. Two more cruisers followed between 1931 and 1935. Thus came *Karlsruhe, Köln*, and *Königsberg; Leipzig* and *Nürnberg*. They could do 32 knots, steam turbines geared in, but they cruised entirely on diesels. Each was slightly different from the previous one, small improvements constantly being made. (See Appendix A.)

At this point, fleet tonnage was still considered limited by Versailles. A number of basic decisions now had to be made, decisions affecting the fundamental role of the new (rebuilt) Navy. Was it to remain a regional "white water" navy, concentrating on coast defense, protection of coastal shipping, and domination of the Baltic? If so, further construction should include a number of coastal battleships—small, slow, but heavily armored and gunned for their size. Or rather, was it again to become a "blue water" world-class navy? If the latter, ocean cruisers were called for. The fleet could not have both. Berlin opted for the latter.

Thus came about the development of the three 10,000-ton, 26-knot (actually 11,700-ton, 28-knot) armored cruisers ("pocket battleships") about which so much is still heard. Armed with six 11-inch guns in two triple turrets, *Deutschland* (eventually renamed *Lützow*), *Admiral Graf Spee*, and *Admiral Scheer* were designed to be able to outrun anything they could not outfight. (At the time, only three British battlecruisers— *Hood, Repulse,* and *Renown*—could do both.) They were powered entirely by diesel, and boasted an enormous range. In naval circles, these caused quite a stir. (Again, see Appendix A.)

Secretly built from German plans drawn in Holland, in Dutch, Spanish, and Finnish yards, a number of prototype U-boats were tested. When in 1935, Hitler's Reich threw over the limitations imposed by the Versailles Treaty, Germany was ready. By 1936, 24 submarines were in commission. By 1939, the now (since 1935) *Kriegsmarine* boasted 57 U-boats, although less than half were combat ready.

In the late 1930s two 26,000-ton battlecruisers appeared—*Scharnhorst* and *Gneisenau*—carrying 11-inch guns. They were followed in the 1940s by two 41,700-ton fast battleships—15-inch-gunned *Bismarck* and *Tirpitz*. Three 14,000-ton, 8-inch-gunned heavy cruisers—unlucky *Blücher*, lucky *Prinz Eugen*, and *Admiral Hipper*—were built, as well. Versailles was done.

THE PLAN Z NAVY

It was in the summer of 1938 (some sources use a Führer conference held in the fall of 1937 as a marker) that Hitler summoned Raeder and informed him that in the long run they would have to fight Britain again. Der Führer wanted the expansion of the Navy speeded up so as to be ready for a conflict he then thought would come in 1944. In the meantime, Raeder could build up his fleet as he wished.

Admiral Raeder and the naval staff developed two large construction programs. The first ("Plan Z") called for the continued development of a balanced ocean fleet, aimed eventually at a capability for sea control. The other program called for concentrating right away on U-boats and pocket battleships, geared for sea denial. Hitler was then offered his choice.

There was only time to complete one of the two plans. Plan Z also required the whole time, the alternative did not. If war came too soon, the sea denial program would still pose a major threat to British communications. It also would, however, preclude Germany's ability to ever face Great Britain on equal terms. If war came early, Plan Z would leave the Reich without a hope of victory at sea.

Hitler opted for Plan Z, noting that the fleet now would not be required before 1946. When in 1939 war actually came, the Navy was thus not

Table 3.1
The *Kriegsmarine*, September 1, 1939

Battlecruisers	2	Scharnhorst and Gneisenau
Fast battleships	2	Bismarck and Tirpitz*
Armored cruisers	3	Deutschland, Scheer, Graf Spee
Heavy cruisers	3	Hipper, Blücher, Prinz Eugen
Light cruisers	5	Königsberg, Nürnberg, Leipzig, Köln, Karlsruhe
Destroyers	22	
Torpedo boats	12	
S-boats	17	
Submarines	57	
Auxiliary cruisers	26	
Training flotilla:		
Old battleships	2	Schlesien, Schleswig-Holstein
Light cruiser	1	Emden

*Not yet operational, almost complete.

ready for either kind of role—against Britain, anyway. Raeder was fully aware of it.

By 1939, the *Kriegsmarine* added up to a fairly balanced if still far from complete fleet. But what use really was it? It was too small to challenge the royal Navy in any kind of fleet action. It was even too weak to launch truly large-scale U-boat and cruiser warfare, by then the only effective alternative that would be open to it. World War II came too soon. Nobody asked the Navy, in any case. (See Table 3.1.)

With this fleet the Germans entered World War II. Still second-best in the Atlantic, the *Kriegsmarine* had little choice now but to resort as best it could to commerce (raider) warfare using its big ships, auxiliary cruisers, and still too few U-boats, in a replay of the previous war. *Graf Spee* ended up scuttling herself at Montevideo before all the world. Radar and sonar one way or the other ensured the doing away of *Bismarck* and *Scharnhorst,* and were containing the submarines. Self-image as a winner cannot be built on that sort of thing.

Work had already been halted on all new buildings except battleships *Bismarck, Tirpitz,* and cruiser *Prinz Eugen,* all three of which were almost complete. This freed the best yards to concentrate on U-boats. But it was already too late.

Once before (1914–1918) in the Baltic the Navy had gained and maintained command of the sea, using it as it wished and denying this to the enemy. But for the Navy the Baltic was a backwater—until 1944 anyway. The Army had begun to use the Navy to ferry supplies (it had not even planned to do that, at first) but that was all. Was this really to be the Navy's fate, ending conceivably with mutiny and another scuttle as before?

NAVAL COMMAND STRUCTURE

The *Kriegsmarine* fought World War II with a carefully thought-out command structure. Based on standard staff and command principles, it was headed by a Commander-in-Chief, Navy. A naval staff provided him strategic and operational (*not* tactical) planning and advice. Together they formed the *Oberkommando der Marine* (OKM). This staff necessarily did have direct control over cruiser warfare in distant waters, including all arrangements for blockade runners and supply ships. It received all foreign intelligence essential to its duties.

OKM looked to be the usual German staff. There was a chief of staff, supervising an operations-heavy general staff known as the *Seekriegsleitung* (SKL). Staff sections included: (1) SKL Organization and Operations; (2) SKL U-boat Operations; (3) SKL Foreign Intelligence; (4) SKL Naval Intelligence; (5) SKL RDF Service. There were others.

There were the administrative and technical staffs and services. Included here were ordnance, administration and supply, construction, and coastal defense.

Directly under Commander-in-Chief, Navy (Erich Raeder, then Karl Dönitz), were the naval group commands, roughly equivalent to U.S. sea frontiers. There was one for the North Sea, another for the Baltic (*Marineoberkommando, Ostsee* [MOK Ost] we shall loosely translate as Naval Group Command, Baltic). After 1940 there was a Norwegian one. These commands controlled the area-wide operating forces. They delegated control of local forces. Naval groups were responsible overall for safety of the coastal waters within their areas, including such matters as surveillance, patrol, minesweeping and minelaying, ASW, and escort duties.

In the Baltic, operations were controlled by Naval High Commander, East—Conrad Albrecht during the Polish war, then Rolf Carls, then finally Oscar Kummetz. These were MOK Ost.

Other senior flag officers were in charge of the various surface fleets, the U-boats, coastal defenses (the Navy defended its own port areas), as well as the Navy's extensive shore set-up.

Below this during the course of the war there was considerable shifting of commands. Assignments depended on the situation. For a while, at the height of Germany's occupation of the Baltic area, there was an Admiral, Baltic, flying his flag at Reval. In the last years, as things began to fall apart, operations in the Baltic were delegated to Admiral, Eastern Baltic, at Danzig, and Western Baltic, at Swinemünde. These officers had functions roughly corresponding to those of naval district commanders in the United States.

THE BIG SHIPS (MAJOR SURFACE COMBATANTS)

The *Kriegsmarine*'s big ships had had a checkered career in the Baltic. There had always been big ships there—the Fleet Training Squadron, new buildings working up, other ships undergoing refit—but no permanent members of a balanced combat fleet, per se. There had been no need for one.

There had been one notable temporary exception to this, in the fall of 1941. To prevent Baltflot from a possible breakout from the Gulf of Finland—mines or no mines—and making west for neutral Swedish ports, thus avoiding either capture by the rapidly advancing *Wehrmacht* or the necessity of blowing themselves up, SKL had formed *Baltenflotte*. This scratch but formidable fleet was made up of new fast battleship *Tirpitz*, armored cruiser *Admiral Scheer*, two light cruisers, three destroyers, a torpedo boat flotilla, and several minelayers. Two additional light cruisers were held in Libau in case of need. This new fleet was positioned in the Aland Sea, on the northern flank of the Gulf exit, ready to pounce on anyone coming out. When no Russian breakout took place, the Baltic Fleet was broken up. That finished that.

At 200700 Aug 44 off Riga, *Prinz Eugen* on a gunfire support mission fired the first ranging shots from her 8-inch guns ever in anger. Little correction was called for. The mission was an entire success. Although *Prinz Eugen* continued to steam at various courses and speeds, her shells were reported as being 80 percent on target.

Meanwhile, *Prinz Eugen*'s escorting four destroyers, temporarily leaving her, moved closer-in themselves to join in the land battle. Their medium guns also did good work, down the coast.

Prinz Eugen and her escorts were soon joined in these missions by *Lützow*, two more destroyers, and two T-boats. This was all to have far-reaching effects on the Baltic battle. In the next nine months more shells were to be fired by the German Navy (against land targets) than had been fired (against ships) in the previous five years. But to understand, again we have to go back a few years.

Der Führer in 1943, only a year and a half earlier, exasperated with his adventures in seapower, had finally ordered the major surface combatants of his fleet decommissioned and broken up. The April 1940 occupation of Norway had been a brilliant example of how control of the sea (even if it was only brief) could clear the way for a naval landing force. But there had of course been costs.

Ten of the most powerful and modern destroyers had landed the occupying force at Narvik, the most northerly of the ports seized by the *Kriegsmarine*. They were all lost defending the port. Also lost during the operation were heavy cruiser *Blücher*, light cruisers *Königsberg* and *Karlsruhe*. *Gneisenau* and *Scharnhorst*—the two new battlecruisers—as well as armored cruiser *Lützow* were seriously damaged.

Operational after Norway were only one heavy cruiser, two light cruisers, and four destroyers—in all the fleet. The Navy was only slowly and expensively rebuilt. Its destroyer force never fully recovered from its losses.

Despite the undoubted overall success of the operation, the Navy had not even there fully exploited its many opportunities for an overwhelming victory. New *Gneisenau* and *Scharnhorst* had failed to push on aggressively against even the Royal Navy's elderly *Renown* when they met her, allowing *Renown* to drive them off, away from the convoys just to her north. Later, after *Scharnhorst* was damaged, *Gneisenau* had broken off her cruise and escorted her sister ship back to port rather than continuing on alone hunting convoys. *Hipper* had left Trondheim too late to catch any at all.

After the seizure of Norway, the *Kriegsmarine* just did not seem to be able to collect itself. There did not seem to be any further use for the big ships—nothing worthwhile, in any case, nothing that worked.

The big ships had not succeeded in closing the critical Atlantic convoy lanes, across which Britain was being sustained. They had not stopped the Russian convoys still going into Murmansk and Archangel around North Cape. Hitler had not been amused by any of this.

In dramatic single ship actions, the fleet even before Norway had lost *Graf Spee* (1939). A year after Norway, it lost *Bismarck* (1941). Both were destroyed by a luckier, more skillful, and harder-fought Royal Navy.

On balance, then, the big surface ships—hamstrung in almost every operation by poor *Luftwaffe* air support—must certainly have seemed to Hitler to have been losers. They had suffered disaster after disaster, it seemed, and looked to do no better. *Gneisenau* had been mined in the dash through the English Channel in February 1942, bombed while in dock in Kiel later that same month, and was never again an operational ship. Her hulk was eventually towed to Gotenhafen, filled with concrete, and sunk, turning her into a blockship fort. *Karlsruhe*, *Königsberg*, *Blücher*, *Graf Spee*, and *Bismarck* just could not be replaced. Except for Norway, the fleet had not visibly achieved nearly as much as had the U-boats, and it cost a whole lot more.

On January 26, 1943, Hitler ordered: "(1) all work on big ships presently in the yards is to cease . . . ; (2) unless required for training purposes, battleships, pocket battleships, heavy and light cruisers are to be decommissioned . . . ; (3) personnel so made available are to work on U-boats."

In view of the political and psychological effect of this order, it was only to be communicated to the smallest number of officers. The news was soon out, in any case.

The Navy saw this order as the equivalent of a great naval victory for Britain. Hitler's order had led to the resignation of Grossadmiral Raeder, and the appointment of Admiral Dönitz to replace him. But Dönitz was fully aware that his U-boats required those big ships at least to defend their bases, and in his indirect way he got what he wanted. "To get along, go along."

The *Seekriegsleitung* thus successfully fended off the worst effects of Hitler's order. Psychologically at least, those big ships were the Navy. Most of them were moved into the Baltic, to become training ships. SKL knew it was a waste, but the need to train U-boat crews was an idea Hitler could grasp. Coincidentally, this had had the lucky effect of putting these ships right in place, ready when their time in history came.

Dönitz even managed to keep *Tirpitz* and *Scharnhorst* operational in northern Norway. Unfortunately, *Scharnhorst* was lost a year later (December 1943) off North Cape, still trying to stop those Russian convoys. *Tirpitz* was sunk in November 1944, on her way back south. By that time, however, the operational need for the remaining big ships (those in the Baltic) had been established beyond question, even for Hitler.

IN THE BALTIC

The German Navy had never experienced the close cooperation with Soviet forces in the 1920s and 1930s enjoyed by the other German armed services. Advances by the Soviets in the Baltic during 1939 and 1940, enabling them to push their bases south, had certainly touched a sensitive naval nerve, but were smoothed over. Naval material promised in 1939 (primarily a half-finished heavy cruiser [the *Seydlitz* hull] and fire control gear) was delivered to the Soviets on schedule. There were no active major professional differences between them. The passion was to come later.

When on June 21, 1941, German forces began hostilities, the *Kriegsmarine* had already begun to lay extensive minefields in the central Baltic. Naval plans called for defensive fields in a belt reaching from Memel—the northernmost port in East Prussia—to near the Swedish island of Öland, to keep the Russians away from German coastal traffic. Some fields were laid farther back, local ones like that off the port of Kolberg in Pomerania. Others were laid more forward, in the mouth of the Finnish Gulf.

This was all done with the relatively scant naval forces already present and ready. The *Kriegsmarine* could always assemble superior forces in the Baltic, through the Kiel Canal or even the Danish Straits. There had been no need then. Only later was a strong Baltic fleet put together—as we have seen—and almost immediately broken up.

In the subsequent course of the war, SKL had set in place an imposing, quite intricate command structure for the Baltic area. With fewer large ships available as the war went on, there were now a larger number of admirals looking for jobs. Up to now, the Baltic had seemed a nice quiet place to put them.

In the summer of 1944, storm clouds looming in the east, a group of senior Baltic flag officers—MOK Ost, flag officer U-boats, and others—met and agreed on the necessity of an overall program for the area. This program consisted of the following measures, apparently not in any priority order:

1. fortification of the Baltic coast;
2. continuation of supply for the Army;
3. adaptation and preparation of additional base facilities for strengthened Baltic naval forces;
4. preparation for evacuation of troops from the north;
5. readying of several strongpoints in the east, i.e., Libau, Memel, Pillau, and Gotenhafen, shifting U-boat training centers there; and
6. transportation of civilians and economically important material out.

The critical factor affecting decisions may have then been that an estimated 50 to 60 percent of U-boat training was carried out in the Baltic. One infantry division had already been brought from Norway to strengthen the Narva front, then being built up.

Events were to overtake some of these measures before they could ever be put into effect, but the flag officers were thinking ahead. The Navy meant to help hold the Ostsee, come what may.

The *Kriegsmarine*'s Baltic command structure got a real workout during 1944, and a number of changes had to be made. With the October loss of steamer *Bremerhaven*, the final Baltic watch bill was essentially written up. In preparation for what was to come, the crew was on board, the watch was set. Exactly what did the watch bill look like?

As reorganized December first, *Generaladmiral* Oscar Kummetz was MOK (High Commander) Ost, based at Kiel. The critical German-controlled Baltic coast was under the direct command of Vice Admiral Theodor Burchardi as Admiral Eastern Baltic, flying his flag at Gotenhafen. There was also an Admiral Western Baltic, with Swinemünde as base. There was still a quasi-autonomous submarine training command, a Fleet Training Squadron, and assorted shore facilities.

The success of *Prinz Eugen* and *Lützow* in their first live shoot after so many sterile years put new spirit into the fleet Training Squadron. The squadron now normally included old battleships *Schlesien* and *Schleswig-Holstein;* armored cruisers *Admiral Scheer* and *Lützow;* heavy cruisers *Prinz Eugen* and *Admiral Hipper;* light cruisers *Nürnberg, Leipzig, Köln,* and *Emden.* From these, as time went on, a number of surface action (combat) groups were drawn. Eventually, all were used up.

The 1st Battle Group (or Force 1) was commanded by Vice Admiral Bernhard Rogge, the 2nd Battle Group (or Force 2) by Vice Admiral August Thiele. To these task groups were attached *Admiral Scheer* and *Lützow,* commanded at this point by Captains Ernst Thienemann and Bodo Knoke, respectively; *Prinz Eugen* and *Admiral Hipper* (until February 1945), commanded by Captains Hans-Jürgen Reinicke and Hans Henigst, as the situation demanded. With escorts of destroyers and torpedo boats, each ship by itself potentially formed the core of its own heavy bombardment group, capable of massive intervention in the ground fight.

As time went on, the battle groups became a frequent and welcome sight along the increasingly unfriendly coast. They operated in support of the Army off such places as Riga, Tukums, the Baltic islands, Windau, Libau, Memel and its port (Cranz), Königsberg (Pillau), the whole Danzig complex, and Kolberg. Bombarding ships had at first to return frequently to port to replenish ammunition and fuel. Soon, however, ships worked in rotation, maintaining continuous support for long periods.

DESTROYERS (Z-BOATS)

Destroyers in this navy were basically gunships with torpedoes. As fleet boats, they normally operated tied to those cruisers. Working under area control, they were home ported like the cruisers at Kiel. They could be, however, and sometimes were assigned as merchant convoy as well as naval escorts, for specific tasks. They themselves provided gunfire support to shore units. As fast minelayers, they were first rate; they carried large numbers and they were in and out of the target area before the enemy knew it.

German destroyers were all post-Versailles designs. Their construction was begun in 1934. The first classes of these destroyers measured around 2230 tons, but this was rapidly increased to 2600. Typically, they mounted five 5.9-inch guns and moved at 36 knots. By 1939, the Navy had 22 of them in service. (See Appendix C.) Ten were lost at Narvik, but their construction was continued. There were never enough of them, in the Navy, either.

These fleet destroyers were obviously big boats for their type, carrying 5.9-inch guns on 2600 tons. U.S. boats did not reach this tonnage until well into World War II. They were sometimes called mini-cruisers and often substituted for them.

To accept these Z-boats as mini-cruisers, however, begs the question. It is too simple a view. These Z-boats did mount 5/9ths of a light cruiser's main battery, but they definitely did not put out 5/9ths of her fire. They lacked a cruiser's higher, dryer, more stable platform; her fire control gear; her ammunition handling gear; and her strong secondary AA battery. They did carry large numbers of 37-mm and 20-mm automatic guns, almost as many light automatic guns as a cruiser.

Although often in harm's way, they were sometimes too valuable to be routinely risked. They were nonetheless ordinarily capable of taking care of themselves. They suffered, however, from continuing problems with their modern high pressure steam propulsion plants, and they were undeniably wet boats.

Z-boats were assigned to the Baltic in 1939, operating against Poland. Three divisions (three boats each) were given Naval Group East. All possible tasks having been quickly satisfied, the boats had shortly then been withdrawn from the Baltic. Even then, they were in short supply, and more needed in the west, facing Britain and France. None were reassigned until Z-Flotilla 6 (some five boats) was moved back in during the spring of 1944. Their numbers increased as the fighting increased in intensity, Z-Flotilla 4 arriving in January 1945. Flotilla 8—essentially an administrative holding unit—was formed later, and was headquartered at Swinemünde.

Z-Flotilla 6 was initially based in the Gulf of Finland, at Reval (and Balticport). Two Z-boats shelled Soviet positions March 12. On June 19, in the Gulf, four of its boats ran into a group of Soviet patrol vessels, soon reinforced by a squadron of torpedo cutters. Nine of the torpedo cutters were destroyed, at no cost to the Z-boats. Z-Flotilla 6 was pulled out of the Gulf in the summer of 1944. By September it was at Gotenhafen, escorting *Prinz Eugen* and *Lützow*. By the end it had been forced back to Kiel.

Apparently available to the Baltic destroyer flotillas at one time or another during 1944 and 1945 were some 14 Z-boats. Baltic operations cost the Navy Z–28, 35, 36, and 43, four of the original five boats. Most of the others received damage.

PRESERVING THE PAST

In mid-January, precious time and a ship were taken out to conserve a piece of the German *volk* past. Light cruiser *Emden* had tied up in

Königsberg, preparatory to undergoing a very much needed engine overhaul. The city was already under siege, artillery muttering in the distance. The cold was intense. Snow was everywhere. Work was slow.

On January 23, overhaul hardly begun, *Emden* was suddenly ordered to cease work and to make all preparations for getting under way as she was. An icebreaker and tugs had been laid on. *Emden's* overhaul would be completed at Kiel. SKL had a special mission for her, nothing less than bringing out the bodies of Field Marshal von Hindenburg and his wife.

The fact was, the Russians could not be allowed to seize the body of the victor of the battle of Tannenberg, nor that of his wife. Salvaged from the Tannenberg memorial just in the nick of time, when the coffins arrived the Field Marshal was accorded all honors. Stowed within a makeshift shelter on the quarterdeck, the coffins were surrounded by a group of old battle flags.

Emden's departure was delayed to allow the Field Marshal's son, General Oscar von Hindenburg, to pay his respects. In the dark, cold, and silently falling snow, in the midst of disaster, it was a moving affirmation that Germany still lived. Von Hindenburg's body lies now in the cathedral at Marburg, along with that of his wife.

GUNFIRE SUPPORT

General shore bombardment the German Navy of course had long known. During the shoot at Riga, however, *Prinz Eugen's* gunnery officer, Lieutenant Commander Paul Schmalenbach, had worked out a new direct gunfire support system. Setting up dedicated radio links, Schmalenbach kept in continuous contact with his spotter aircraft, artillery forward observers, and the spearhead units of the tank column he was supporting. His guns were immediately responsive to requests for fire. Fire was adjusted, and shifted, as called for. Joint gunfire support radio nets became standard for all the battle groups.

At 1500 meters, a destroyer's 5.9-inch guns proved murderous against individual Soviet tanks and other point targets. The cruisers' guns were more used at longer ranges for shoots at area targets, against which their guns were equally deadly. They were especially good at counter-battery fire, those bigger guns.

At Riga, the cruisers had been helping hold open a narrow 30-mile choke point through which the retreating *Wehrmacht* had to pass. Through this gap 29 Army divisions, 2 brigades, 190 AA batteries, 28 separate artillery units, and 68 pioneer battalions, with over 111,000 vehicles, streamed west, finally to form and hold the Kurland pocket. It would never have existed without them. It could not have been held without them.

Even with its back to the sea, the Army could now hold its ground, at least for a while. Naval gunfire could check the Soviet advance, though it could not by itself ever permanently halt it. That took sufficient troops, and they were just no longer to be had.

As winter arrived in the Baltic, the emphasis of naval gunfire support shifted somewhat. Ships continued bombardment in support of the various pockets, of course. But more and more, the call was for fire in support of pockets of refugees—not troops per se—and their evacuation points. Ships' AA capabilities gained accordingly in value. They were all there was.

As the fighting on land continued, most of the road and rail networks deteriorated for one reason or another. They were overused and undermaintained. They were choked with refugees. They were blown up, or at least cut. Sea lines of communication (SLOCs) became increasingly matters of prime importance. There was more traffic than ever at sea.

Also participating in the Navy's gunfire support role were a number of improvised, less glamorous ships. There were improvised monitors like *Nienburg*, a 400-ton Dutch-built motor coaster converted into a "heavy artillery carrier," not a beautiful but undoubtedly a useful support ship.

The longer the evacuation from the east went on, the more destructive became Soviet air power, and the less capable the *Luftwaffe* to defend against it. The *Kriegsmarine* therefore also improvised flak-ships like *Arcona*, a converted old light cruiser of 2706 tons, rebuilt to carry five heavy (105-mm) as well as an array of smaller AA guns.

NOT IN VAIN

The *Kriegsmarine*'s major surface combatants—they had barely survived threats to relegate them to the scrap heap—had, then, in the Baltic finally found themselves a major role. Through just their simple existence, they provided necessary distant cover to the operations of all of the Navy's lesser ships and craft, neutralizing a superior Soviet fleet. Putting their guns to other uses (gunfire support) they bought the Army probably an extra year in which to salvage what it could from the clearly inevitable debacle in the east. They gave close cover to the exodus of the Balts and the wounded from the east—not in vain.

To these big ships is credited the success of the Kurland armies, enabling the *Wehrmacht* to hold its large pocket around Libau and Windau right to the end. The ships' big guns repeatedly shelled Red Army units assembling for the attack, and broke them up.

To these ships is credited the fact that Memel—on the south (other) side of the Soviet breakthrough—was held from October 1944 until January 1945. The Navy had a special relationship with Memel. Memel had been a border port of 40,000, lost by Germany to Lithuania after Versailles. In March 1939, it was re-occupied from the sea by a naval task group. The entire operation was mounted and led by Hitler and Raeder personally, in *Deutschland*. They had been welcomed by a delirious city.

To these ships is credited also the long successful defense of the vital Danzig Bay complex. By March, Battle Group "Rogge" (*Prinz Eugen, Schlesien, Leipzig*, and escorts) was on almost permanent station there. "Rogge" was frequently reinforced by Battle Group "Thiele" (*Lützow* and destroyers), down to the end. Without this complex for the reception and shipment or transshipment of evacuees, many fewer would have made it from the east.

To these ships is credited the temporary defense of many of the beaches used to extract isolated groups of fleeing refugees as well as troops, up and down the coast.

Throughout, the always sufficient normal hazards of navigation at sea remained, themselves threats to every vessel, merchant or naval. All the war did was to add its own kind of dangers on top of the other. In October off Hela, at night and in fog, *Prinz Eugen* rammed *Leipzig* right amidship, almost cutting her in half. Following widely accepted damage control procedures, *Prinz Eugen* kept her bow jammed in the hole, supporting *Leipzig*. Although helpless to defend themselves, the two immobile ships were not attacked. They were kept afloat. The two remained fixed together for 14 hours while bulkheads were shored up and emergency patches readied. *Prinz Eugen* took only two weeks to repair, but *Leipzig* was never fully operational again.

Hipper's withdrawal in February was a command decision. She was worn out, no longer operationally fully fit. She had been damaged in earlier operations, the effects of which she still showed. She badly needed new barrel liners for her guns as well as extensive work on her boilers. She was short of crew. In any case, she was a heavy consumer of fuel; her oil could probably be better used by others. Docking *Hipper* in Kiel was a calculated risk Dönitz was probably prepared to lose. Lose it he did—British bombs wrecked her there.

Nürnberg was pulled out at some point, to be used as a fast minelayer in the North Sea and the Skagerrak. The door to the Baltic had to be kept shut, still. The Norway SLOC had to be kept open. Reseeding and extending existing fields now took something big enough and strong enough to operate under hostile air. *Nürnberg* was the one. She survived the war.

The *Kriegsmarine* lost not one of its big ships *at sea* here through hostile action, although they were heavily and steadily attacked from the air. Major ships in lesser states of readiness acted as fortress ships, fixed gun platforms off various defended areas, as long as they could. They were lost. So were those caught in dockyard hands.

4

District and Escort Forces

"SECURITY" FORCES

While as usual the big ships got most of the glory, here too lesser ships and craft played their necessary and sometimes, in some ways, larger roles. In the United States these are usually known as district and escort forces, as opposed to fleet units.

Admirals Burchardi (Admiral, Eastern Baltic) and Lange (Admiral, Western Baltic) had in the last months direct control of what the *Kriegsmarine* called "security" forces—assorted minesweepers, motor minesweepers, submarine chasers, and escorts as assigned by task. These forces were, as their name implies, responsible for securing coastal waters, for making and keeping them usable. The defeat in France and the withdrawal from northern Norway freed significant additional numbers of these types, most of which were transferred to the Baltic and received by Burchardi.

How were these lesser ships and craft organized? How were they commanded? Why? What did they actually do?

Working under the Baltic admirals were two security (minesweeping and escort) divisions. The 9th Division (Commander [later Rear Admiral] Adalbert von Blanc) was based first entirely at Reval, watching over the Gulf of Finland; then as the *Wehrmacht* was pushed back, at Reval, Windau, and Libau; then at Pillau and Gotenhafen; and last at Hela.

Beginning in December, there was a 10th Division (Commander Hugo Heydal), based at Swinemünde.

Experienced Escort Division 9 had responsibility for Hela and the waters from the western shores of the Gulf of Danzig east to Kurland. It controlled three flotillas of M-boats (each with half a dozen operational ships); two of R-boats; plus an assortment of trawlers, drifters, and other auxiliaries. The 10th was responsible for inshore waters on the north German coast, including the stretch from Rixhöft, just west of Danzig, west to the Danish islands. It disposed of a similar force.

On February first, Admiral, Eastern Baltic, took over actual local direction of evacuation transport from Seetra. With responsibility for escort to and from two main collecting and transshipment ports, Danzig and Pillau, his 9th Escort Division effectively split its command structure in two. Von Blanc set up a forward staff in Windau, remaining there. In Gotenhafen, Lieutenant Commander Wolfgang Leonhardt ran the 9th's small operations office in von Blanc's name. His staff in the map and radio room consisted of five officers and a handful of enlisted men. This small group was responsible for naval control of shipping and escort management in an operational area which extended at its height for some 700 miles, taking in thousands of people and dozens of ships. Leonhardt there plotted intelligence of hostile forces, setting convoy schedules and routes so as best to avoid them. He tracked the convoys as they moved and directed the minesweepers, keeping the merchantmen and naval auxiliaries to safe channels, somehow keeping ahead of a seemingly tireless enemy.

District and escort forces—all types—torpedo boats, motor torpedo boats (S-boats), minesweepers and other light craft, were organized into flotillas (roughly equivalent to U.S. squadrons). Strengths varied widely, with need, and with availability of ships. Numbers indicated here are the theoretical ones, at full strength. These were seldom the real world case, especially in the Baltic's last days. Flotillas were tactical as well as administrative units. They fought a steady guerrilla war with the opposing light forces. Escorts, as always and everywhere in this war, were in short supply.

Here, the Russian (and later British) mines, torpedoes, guns, and bombs inevitably took a continuing toll. Equipment began to deteriorate with hard service, and could not be repaired or replaced. Yet the necessary shipping lanes were kept usably open and convoys somehow escorted until the very end. And beyond. The flotillas earned their pay.

NAVAL PERSONNEL

Until 1935 the German Navy had been limited in its personnel by the Versailles Treaty. The treaty allowed it a strength of 100,000, of whom

1500 could be officers. Enlisted men volunteered for 12-year periods, officers served for 25. Annual turnover was not to exceed 5 percent. A reserve had been forbidden, remember. This all did make for a number of problems at the time, but it also provided a superb pool of highly trained, eminently promotable regulars in case of need. Lieutenants were embryo commanders, and so on.

In 1935 Versailles was denounced. The Navy began overtly to expand. A large increase in personnel was going to be required to man its new ships. Where to find them? Universal conscription was re-introduced; the Navy received a share of each intake. Midshipmen classes rose sharply. A number of carefully chosen, experienced merchant service officers were integrated into the officer corps. There was a certain amount of promotion from within, too.

Simultaneously, interested officers from World War I, other merchant officers, and yachtsmen ("mahogany lieutenants") were sent through short refresher courses and commissioned in a recreated reserve. World War II came before this system had reached its stride, however, and they were still many too few. It was the small ships and craft that paid.

When World War II came, the Navy had to requisition, buy, or build a host of yet additional small ships and craft for minesweeping, patrol, and the like. Because of the relatively inelastic technical requirements of the big ships and the continuing Navy-wide shortage of trained man-power, many of these ships and craft—particuarly those brought up from the fishing fleet—had initially to be manned by crews without previous naval technical training. Adding new recruits did not much help.

To help overcome the continuing personnel shortage (especially on those smaller ships and craft) additional officers and petty officers were called out of retirement. Men with service in World War I were called up from civilian life. These were given short refreshers and put back to work. Not everyone could have been enchanted with this.

The whole was carefully leavened with a scattering of those scarce regulars—officers, petty officers, and men—with the result that the *Kriegsmarine* not only soon became one homogeneous force, but also a good reflection of the whole German people. In the final analysis, it was but a piece of them. This was a great achievement, and would pay off well.

With bitter memories of 1918's mutinies well in mind—these were like death at the feast—the Navy paid careful attention to its personnel policies. Officers and petty officers were instructed and re-instructed in techniques of leadership. On the big ships in 1918, food had been a major issue. This time everyone ate the same food prepared in the same galley. Discipline remained strict, standards high.

This time, naval leadership worked. There was never at any time to be a general breakdown of discipline such as occurred before. Rather, the Navy's personnel structure was to stand proudly up to every stress right to the end.

TORPEDO CRAFT

Torpedo boats (T-boats) and *Schnellboote* (motor torpedo boats, or S-boats) were cousins. Just as the T-boats developed into mini-destroyers (destroyer escorts in the United States), so the S-boats developed into substitute torpedo boats. Both types here were and remained primarily torpedo carriers, their guns intended essentially to perform only a defensive role. Both played a major part in operations in the Ostsee.

While the major combatants—cruisers and destroyers, here—were undeniably essential in the Baltic, they were really only big "blue water" ships that had come in from the cold. The torpedo craft (T-boats and S-boats) were made to order as if for Baltic coastal warfare, and did just as important work. First, a look at T-boats:

Torpedo boats varied widely in size, perhaps more than any other type. They measured as little as 850 tons (early boats) through 950 to as much as 1400 tons (later fleet boats). Characteristically, they carried 4.1-inch guns and an assortment of light AA weapons, as well as torpedoes and, on occasion, mines. For their size, they were good sea boats. They sometimes suffered from the lightness of their gun fit—too light for the English Channel or the Norwegian leads—but they were ideal for the Ostsee. (See Appendix C.)

Of relatively shallow draft, handy sized, T-boats were found on every hand, in the Ostsee, if in varying numbers, right from 1939. By the close of 1943, all of those operational were assigned to the Baltic, or were there in dockyard hands, or were working up there. Not all were used as torpedo boats. Most of the older boats were employed for a while as torpedo retrievers and the like. But as things got tight, they reverted to type.

By 1944, T-Flotillas 2, 3, 5, and 6, based at Reval, Windau, Libau, and Gotenhafen were carrying the brunt of the inshore escort load. When after only six months the destroyers were pulled back out of the Finnish Gulf, too valuable to be any longer risked there, T-Flotilla 6 stayed behind. They, too, were finally driven off.

By 1945, there were only 12 operational T-boats left in the Baltic. T-Flotilla 2 had four boats, 3 (at Libau) had three, and 5 had three (two boats were working detached in the Skagerrak). T-Flotilla 6 had been decommissioned in October.

Compared with destroyers, they were expendable and they were almost as useful. They substituted for Z-boats. They escorted. They patrolled, targets for whatever came along. They carried refugees. They laid mines.

T–3 and T–5 were sunk by mines at Hela. T–34 was lost in the central Baltic. T–36 was finished off from the air after she had been damaged by a mine. T–10 was destroyed by a bomb while in dock at Gotenhafen. Seven others were also lost in the Baltic. (See Appendix E.)

S-boats provided an offensive arm for local naval area commanders, filling a true torpedo boat role. The *Kriegsmarine* was one of the few navies to enter the war with well designed and tested operational motor torpedo boats and a well thought out doctrine for using them. The Baltic had always been in turmoil, it seemed, and had to be patrolled. S-boats appeared the answer. Germany had already been making good use of them.

S-boats carried at least two torpedoes (21-inchers), six mines or two reload torpedoes, and a quite substantial array of light automatic guns. With their characteristic in-hull forward-firing torpedo tubes, they were large for their type (114-feet long). They were diesel powered (making them difficult to set on fire) and reasonably fast (39-plus knots). (See Appendix C.)

S-boats were famously good sea boats, for their type. They had displacement hulls and, at 100 tons, they were roughly twice the size of other such craft. They proved employable in weather up to Beaufort Force 5, even in the Ostsee's short steep seas. When necessary, they could transport up to 30 or 40 people, evacuees or troops—very maneuverable they were, too.

After an initial concentration against Poland in 1939, and against Russia in 1941—for a short while, the bulk of the operational S-Flotillas (1, 2, 3, 5, 6) worked there—the Baltic numbers were drawn down. Between autumn 1941 and spring 1944, no S-boat served in the Finnish Gulf, for instance. But then their strength was again quickly built up, in response to the growing crisis. There were three flotillas in the Ostsee at the end.

Manned by many of the Navy's natural fighters, S-boats as a rule operated by flotilla (basically, six boats) or half flotilla. They did not hesitate to take on major combatants, sinking destroyer *Smely* early in the war. They endlessly fought their own kind. In particularly dangerous waters they escorted convoys. They laid mines. Although details are not available, it is clear that they raised havoc with enemy coastal traffic, merchant and naval.

Each flotilla was based on a tender—typically a 3100-ton converted cargo ship. These tenders carried fuel, ammunition, torpedoes, food, and water. They could undertake repairs. They provided accommodation for the crews, and a target ship for practice runs. They carried the flotilla staff and furnished them with office space.

MINE WARFARE CRAFT

Minesweepers (M-boats) and motor minesweepers (R-boats) were another common sight in the Baltic. These ubiquitous craft were forever quietly mine hunting, sweeping and check sweeping, endlessly working up and down the traffic lanes, in the harbor approaches, and within the ports. Just to see that they had enough to do, when they were not sweeping mines, they laid them, as well.

These mine warfare craft were a handy size—600 tons for the M-boats, 125 for the R-boats. Well designed, with excellent seakeeping qualities for their size, they could work up a good turn of speed (16–20 knots). Standardized designs had been developed and the hulls were turned out in large numbers. (Something on the order of 400 R-boats were turned out.) These military designs were reinforced with large numbers of auxiliary sweepers. Fishing trawlers (natural sweepers) were converted and used in quantity, too. (With the war, many commercial fishing boats became available. The Allied blockade closed off many traditional fishing grounds.)

The smaller minesweepers were generally organized on paper at least into flotillas of nine operational boats—four pairs plus a buoy boat. There was a flotilla office ashore. Each sweeper carried one or more guns, Oropesa (adjustable depth moored mine) sweep gear, a hydrophone, and depth charges—by 1944, in any case. They frequently laid mines as well as swept them. (See Appendix E.)

Not all minesweepers were always employed as sweepers, however. Sweepers were relatively plentiful. Escorts were not, and the need for them was growing fast. Sweepers made very useful escorts, especially when their cumbersome sweep gear was stowed or even landed and stored ashore, and they were provided additional depth charges, listening devices, and guns.

Minesweepers—especially the auxiliary trawlers—were frequently employed as patrol boats. They secured harbor entrances and their approaches offshore. They patrolled minefields and nets. Ordinarily, in friendly waters, since there were so many of them, there was always the dark silhouette of one or more somewhere on the horizon.

Attrition rates among minesweepers were high. The mines themselves got many of them. No mine clearance was ever 100 percent effective. The sweepers themselves hit mines for which they were searching, either because one had escaped the sweeps or because one had broken loose from its moor and was adrift. Or the sweepers—equipped primarily for contact sweeping—ran into mixed fields and set off an influence mine.

The sweepers also suffered continually and inescapably from air attack. Tied either to their sweep gear in the middle of a minefield or to a convoy, their room for maneuver was somewhat limited. Their AA armament could never be sufficient to keep the attacking planes at a safe distance, but they ended up carrying lots of it. Enough ammunition for a long defense could never be carried.

The Baltic being frequently so very shallow, sweeping with M- or even R-boats was often an impossible task. The Navy early developed special mine clearance ships for just this purpose. Typically, these were converted former merchant vessels on the order of say 5100 GRT, armed with three 4.1-inch guns, carrying around a dozen motor pinnaces equipped for the actual clearance of mines in shallow water. The mother ship would lay off in deeper cleared water, launch her pinnaces, orchestrate their effort, and give them cover. These ships were kept busy.

Not even a quick survey of German mine warfare such as this would be complete without a mention of the *Sperrbrecher*. The word is not usefully translatable. These were also unique mine clearance vessels, medium-sized degaussed ex-cargo ships the bows of which had been powerfully electrified. Capable of setting off magnetic influence-activated mines ahead before reaching them, these ships were mobile electromagnets. Every port had at least one. *Sperrbrechers* preceded all important large entering and existing vessels.

With *Sperrbrechers,* especially sensitive to self-generated magnetism, armament was a trade-off. As a rule, they carried no defenses of their own. Theirs was a spine-jarring task. Damage was frequent.

Considerble thought had been devoted to the manning of these mine warfare craft. During the prewar expansion of the Navy, selected reserve officers and short-service crews had been regularly assigned to sweepers for training. By 1939 there had been a significant reserve ready to help man the auxiliary sweepers that were brought into service.

Minesweeper commanding officers and their squadron commanders were regularly chosen from officers who had already served in sweepers. Emphasis was on "fleeting up." This made maximum use of their hard-earned experience as well as building up a dedicated minesweeper service. The system worked well.

INSHORE CRAFT

This war was above all fought by the "white water" and, its shadow, the "brown water" navies. In the Baltic, high premium was always placed on vessels able to work along an almost invariably shallow coast, close inshore, from small fishing ports, and the like. This led to the development and wide use of a variety of specialized logistic and combat craft, as well as a greatly expanded role for S-boats, R-boats, trawlers, drifters, and tugs.

Conventional "war transports" were developed—emergency coastal freighters of 700 tons, 12 knots, and up to 400 tons of crago. They were quite cheap, easy to build, handy, and expendable—ugly, too, but exceedingly useful.

So were ferry-barges, or F-lighters, technically called *Marinefährprähme* (MFPs). These were landing craft, self-propelled barges of about 170 tons, capable of making 11 knots. Of shallow draft, with wide, flat, open decks, MFPs could carry three trucks or 100 tons of cargo, or some combination thereof. Being flat bottomed, they could run up on a beach, lower their bow ramps, and immediately start loading or discharging their cargo. MFPs were widely used to transport personnel, wheeled and tracked vehicles, and artillery. They carried ammunition and stores. Some 62 MFPs worked in the Baltic—24 L-Flotilla in Kurland, 11 L-Flotilla in north Germany—ferrying between ship and shore or between nearby ports.

From these gun-barges grew ferry-barges mounting 88- or 195-mm guns and an array of AA guns. These were used for landing craft escort, close-in shore bombardment, and everything else. Some even laid mines or worked at ASW.

There were mass-produced *Siebelfähre* (Siebel-ferries). These 90-foot by 50-foot, 190-ton tank landing craft were built from two Dutch barges joined by a bridge deck. They had a draft of only 40 inches, no freeboard to speak of and a range of only 160 miles. Two automobile engines gave them a speed of only 7 knots. In their basic configuration, they carried two 20-mm light automatic guns, but they could carry 88- and 37-mm guns, troops, or cargo.

There were "fish cutters" (KFKs), general purpose small (60–80 tons) patrol boats built on a trawler hull and engine. They were wooden hulled, of course, to make use of the many small, otherwise unemployed, outport yards.

Inevitably these small craft suffered from limitations. Patrol often required them to reach offshore and then to loiter for sometimes long periods of time, then fight. Transport demanded that they move troops or cargo over distance in all states of sea. But the basic endurance of these craft was usually measured in terms of hours. In seas as rough as a state 5 or 6, crew endurance might be measured in terms of only minutes, at best.

These small craft were almost all Navy manned. The Army contributed pioneer boats. It was dangerous work. Not only was pilotage and dead reckoning in the shallows and shifting sand banks a difficult art, at best, there was also the ice. And there was the enemy, who fought the same kind of inshore war. The men coped, in any case. (See Table 4.1.)

INSHORE WARFARE

For the Germans and their Finnish allies, the main naval task in all those early years had been to prevent Soviet submarines out of Lenin-

Table 4.1
Key Naval Vessels Engaged in Baltic*

Armored cruisers	2	Deutschland and Scheer
Heavy cruisers	2	Prinz Eugen and Hipper
Light cruisers	4	Nürnberg, Leipzig, Köln,
		Emden
Old battleships	2	Schlesien, Schleswig-Holstein
Destroyers	14	
Torpedo boats	24	
S-boats	20	
M-boats	36	
R-boats	32	
Auxiliary cruisers	5	
Armed trawlers	30	
MFPs (ferry-barges)	62	

*Altogether, a total of some 400 naval units have been identified. Only the most significant have been listed here.

grad from attacking their vital traffic in the Baltic proper. In 1942 alone, the Germans had escorted nearly 1900 merchantmen, reportedly totaling 5.6 million tons. Over 400,000 troops had been transported forward by sea. The *Wehrmacht* (read Army) had outrun its own supply capability, and had rediscovered the possibilities of sea transport, once again.

The German high command was not yet *in extremis*, and was quite prepared to allocate whatever resources were needed to retain control of the Baltic, at that point. Their attitude was grounded on three reasons: across the Baltic came high grade iron ores and specialty steels (including ball bearings) from Sweden, things Germany badly needed (eleven million tons of high grade iron ores were brought down from Sweden annually, most via Lulea until the Gulf of Bothnia froze over, then via Narvik and the Norwegian leads); the *Kriegsmarine* also trained its crews in the relatively quiet Baltic; and, the Army needed the Baltic SLOCs for seaborne supply, to Finland as well as Kurland.

Convoying nonetheless soaked up a considerable number of ever-scarce assets. But the Germans could not do without it. In 1942, after the ice had cleared, there were always two or three Soviet submarines at large in the Baltic, and occasionally up to five. They made 24 attacks on shipping, 17 of which were against convoys. They managed to sink seven ships (about 20,000 tons) with torpedoes; five were damaged, and one small vessel was sunk by gunfire. Finnish submarines torpedoed two Soviet submarines and rammed a third. Mines got an unknown number more.

To close the Soviet submarine route down the Gulf of Finland entirely, German net layers under a Captain Tschirch ran a double antisubmarine net across the Gulf in the spring of 1943. These nets extended north from the Estonian coast west of Reval to the Finnish coast near Porkkala. That did the job. The net was relaid after the ice in 1944. From then on, as long as the nets could be held, not one Soviet submarine succeeded in passing through. Convoying was stopped. Not one ship was lost as a result.

In any case, a lively guerrilla war continued in the Gulf, fought by the opposing light forces. Mines were laid and swept. Raids were carried out. Islands were stormed—and held or lost. Minesweepers and S-boats, especially, had little peace.

MARKING THE NAVY

A word, then, about the personnel manning the inshore forces. It was their performance which was the real test of the *Kriegsmarine*, especially in light of the precedent set back in 1918. It was they who stamped the Navy what it really was, for better or worse—they who would call it quits.

There were the men who routinely manned the hundreds of small craft—fish cutters, F-lighters, tugs, launches, patrol boats of every description, even row boats. Without fuss, under continuous fire, they performed the myriad minor but indispensable inshore tasks in Kurland, Pillau, Danzig, and elsewhere.

Think of the courage of the coxswains of the MFPs and the skippers of the fishing boats who in cold sweat put into shore around Danzig Bay, searching for people needing help. None could ever be sure that it was not a Soviet tank or carefully sited machine gun that waited instead for them. Despite these dangers, they went on in.

There were the minesweeper crews. If sweepers themselves hit a mine, the engineers could all expect to die. If they were machine gunned from the air, the deck gangs perished. The war was patently almost over. They kept on to the end and beyond.

One typical surface action began March 26, 1945, when Soviet planes attacked a small loaded fuel tanker escorted by four R-boats on her way from Pillau to Libau. The enemy planes sank the precious, irreplaceable tanker and three of her escorts before *Luftwaffe* fighters arrived and shot down 11 of the enemy. Three S-boats out of Libau under Lieutenant Hans-Helmut Klose picked up the survivors, took them to base, then returned to the still-burning tanker.

During the night Klose completely surprised nine Soviet torpedo cut-

2 The Gulf of Finland

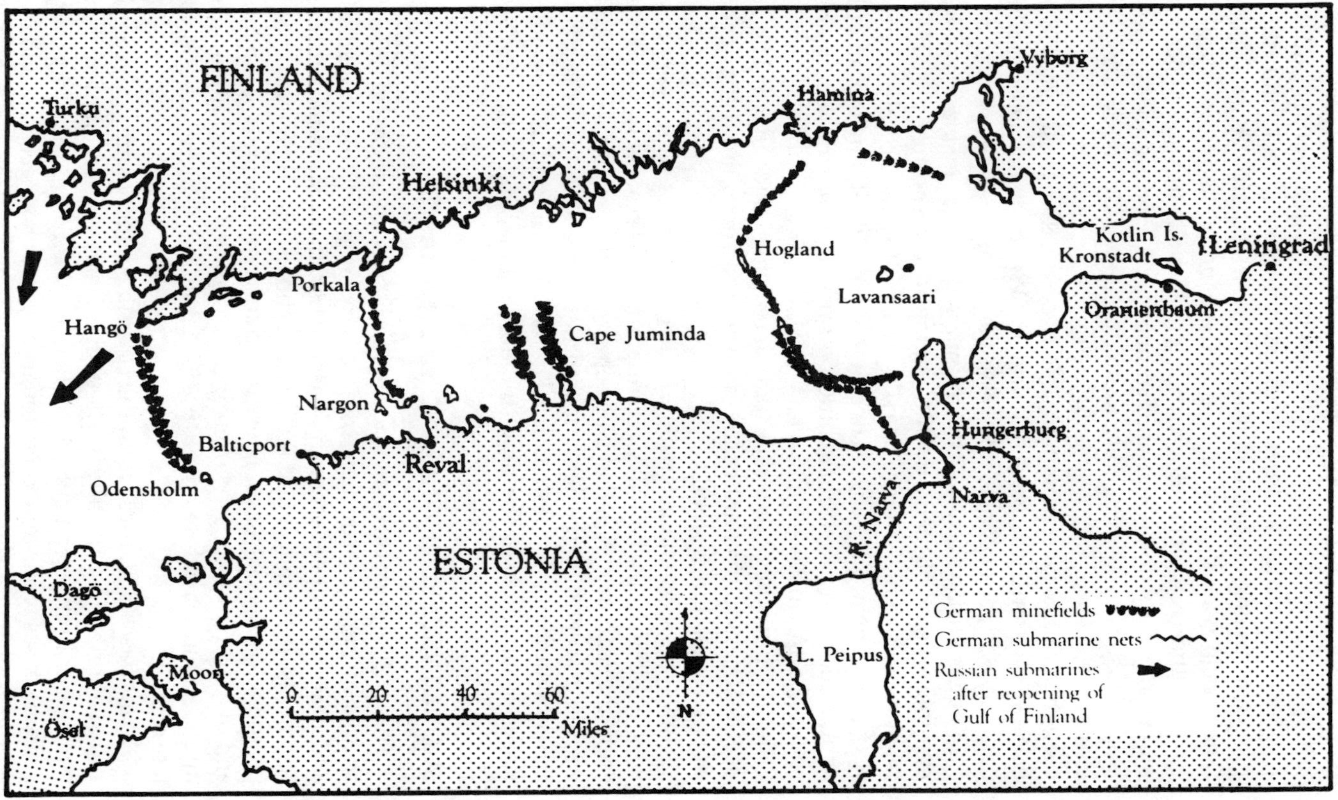

FINLAND

Turku

Hangö

Porkala

Helsinki

Hamina

Viborg

Kotlin Is.
Kronstadt
Oranienbaum

Hungerburg

Narva

Narva

L. Peipus

Hogland

Lavansaari

Cape Juminda

Nargon

Reval

Balticport

Odensholm

Dago

Moon

Ösel

ESTONIA

German minefields
German submarine nets
Russian submarines
after reopening of
Gulf of Finland

N

0   20   40   60
Miles

ters looking for signalbooks or other salvageable material. In a fight lasting two hours, waged at 300 meters, the three S-boats sank two of the enemy, boarded another one, and took five officers and nine men prisoner. Among those taken was the Soviet squadron commander. One S-boat sailor was slightly injured in the action. The fuel was lost.

Ships and craft were tethered for long periods to known locations or moved regularly down known channels in close proximity to prominent landmarks. They were readily located and steadily attacked by the enemy.

Night actions were common, radar or no. On these craft in these waters, everyone was on a hair trigger. When challenged, one had to be ready with a response, answering at once, or else.

In these surface actions, the primary task was to place the largest possible weight of metal on the enemy in the shortest possible time. Inshore craft were therefore heavily armed. Sustained combat, however, was for them not feasible. There were strict limits on the amount of ammunition (and fuel) that could be carried on board. Actions blazed suddenly up, and were almost as quickly over.

But the fundamental naval situation remained unchanged. The Soviet fleet had ceased to count as an important factor in the Baltic seapower equation—as things stood.

However, as is characteristic in such theaters of war, events ashore were about to impact forcibly on the situation at sea. As we have already seen, the seapower equation was being eroded by external events. Storm warnings were flying. The mine and net barriers could not last beyond the sufferance of Baltflot, now. The crucial question was, would the *Kriegsmarine* adjust to the new situation in time, and with what?

SHORE INSTALLATIONS AND UNITS—BASES

The *Kriegsmarine* consisted not only of ships and men, but also of an always surprising assortment of necessary shore activities, installations, and units. First there were the bases. Then there were recruit training regiments, petty officer and technician schools, and regiments grouping personnel for special tasks. There were naval artillery units, conventional and AA, running loosely from brigade down to detachment in size, intended for coastal defense. In the last months, there were naval infantry units.

Taking bases first, these form the essential military joint between shore and sea, providing naval vessels with logistic support (replenishment, replacement, and repair) and shelter. In the Baltic, the *Kriegsmarine*'s wartime bases (determined by geography) were of necessity widely dispersed. The main relatively ice-free bases on the eastern coast were Pillau and Königsberg, and Libau. Bases subject to severe icing during the

Table 4.2
Kriegsmarine's Baltic Bases

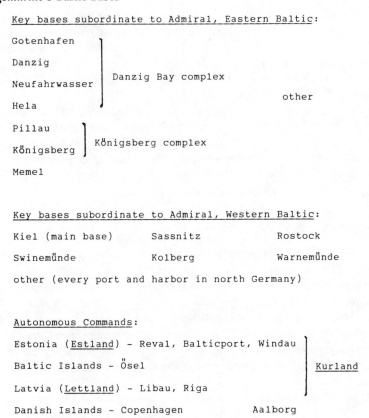

Key bases subordinate to Admiral, Eastern Baltic:

Gotenhafen ⎫
Danzig ⎪
Neufahrwasser ⎪ Danzig Bay complex
Hela ⎭   other

Pillau ⎫
Königsberg ⎪ Königsberg complex
Memel ⎭

Key bases subordinate to Admiral, Western Baltic:

Kiel (main base)   Sassnitz   Rostock

Swinemünde   Kolberg   Warnemünde

other (every port and harbor in north Germany)

Autonomous Commands:

Estonia (Estland) - Reval, Balticport, Windau ⎫
Baltic Islands - Ösel   ⎬   Kurland
Latvia (Lettland) - Libau, Riga   ⎭

Danish Islands - Copenhagen   Aalborg
                 Apenrade   Aarhus

winter were Riga and Reval. Along the south coast were the Danzig complex, Swinemünde, and Kiel. Kiel was of course still the principal German Baltic base. (See Table 4.2.)

Finland while an ally offered the valuable Turku, Hangö, and Helsinki.

By 1944, Reval (inside and on the south shore of the Finnish Gulf, seized in 1941) had been developed into quite a sizable German forward base, ice or no. From it, the Gulf's mine and net barriers could relatively easily be serviced and defended. Much of the guerrilla war being fought between the opposing light forces took place practically in front. Reval was a major convoy terminus and escort base. Balticport just to the west was effectively annexed to the base. Until 1944, operations during the ice season were forced to taper off, anyhow, on both sides. Reval's loss in September was felt.

By November 1944, with Reval again in enemy hands, Windau and Libau under siege, naval forces had to be pulled back and all major units were now home-based. This meant a voyage of as much as 450 miles to the entrance of the Finnish Gulf, and only a little less to Windau or Libau, where once these had been nearby operational areas. This added considerably to operational strain.

Of temporary advanced base locations—temporary and less than complete almost by definition—there were plenty: every fishing village or lumber port's small harbor, the lee of almost any small island, every fjord and cove. Here, the presence of a tender and perhaps a small tanker were a sine qua non. Such bases were most often pushed forward to support U-boats and light forces.

OTHER SHORE-BASED UNITS

The Soviet Navy favored raids, landing parties of up to battalion strength. These were mostly just pieced-together operations, but they could and did threaten German shore positions, by blowing up facilities, collecting intelligence, seizing prisoners, and creating diversions, if nothing else. Lacking radar or sufficient patrol planes, the German Navy countered by setting up a network of early warning observation posts, to monitor coastal traffic from the shore. This at the same time provided them the capability of following their own coastal traffic, and of assisting in search and rescue.

Not all naval gunfire support was provided by ships. A most important fraction was provided on land. The Navy ashore included fixed coast artillery, mobile regular artillery, light and heavy AA units. These were to defend both the Navy's own bases and their companion commercial ports. (Normally, the Army was responsible for defending all coastal areas not directly the responsibility of the Navy. This implied the existance of mobile defense units which in the last months the Army did not have.) As fighting neared the coast, these artillery units gave extensive support to the Army. More and more in demand, many units were organized as late as 1945 to help defend areas not originally in need of them.

All of these various shore activities were coordinated by a series of naval commandants subordinate to Admirals, Eastern and Western Baltic. Basically, there was such a commandant for each coastal German land—East and West Prussia, Pomerania, Mecklenburg, Schleswig-Holstein—Kurland and the Danish Islands.

With the advance of the Allies into Germany proper, shore personnel that became excess were formed into naval infantry divisions. These helped defend the naval ports and even reinforced the fighting front, buying a few more hours. Others were formed into garrison battalions, relieving Army units for service at the front. The naval infantry fought well, but their lack of field experience resulted in their taking heavy losses.

NAVAL AIR

Only in 1939, after much political infighting, did the *Kriegsmarine* and the *Luftwaffe* reach the agreement which governed their wartime roles and missions. Under it, anything that flew belonged to the *Luftwaffe*. The *Kriegsmarine* was to exercise operational control of over-water air reconnaissance, and tactical air operations during contact between naval forces. The *Luftwaffe* retained control of all else: aerial minelaying, air strikes against shipping both in harbor and at sea, air strikes on shipyards and bases.

The *Luftwaffe* was to organize, train, and equip the following dedicated maritime air units: 9 squadrons of flying boats; 18 multipurpose ASW, bombing, and torpedo squadrons; and 2 squadrons of catapult planes. Only half of these were ever organized, in the event. Neither over-water air reconnaissance nor air strike nor combat air defense was ever adequate.

The best possible (more powerful, faster) maritime aircraft were never developed. *Luftwaffe* radio frequencies and codes did not mesh with the Navy's. Air-delivered sea mines were badly designed. The Air Force preferred to use bombs against ships, the Navy torpedoes. The *Luftwaffe* converted only too late to the naval view. So it went.

Luftwaffe-controlled aircraft tender *Hans-Albrecht Wedel* with three Arado float-equipped observation planes long lay off Windau. The Arados performed gunfire spotting as well as ASW patrols around the big ships. "Germany's only aircraft carrier" was much loved. Too soon, however, both planes and fuel were gone.

German maritime air thus plays only a small part in our story. Cooperation between the two services was never very good. In any case, by the time the locus of naval action shifted to the Baltic, the *Luftwaffe* was less and less capable of intervening in the fight. Attrition was taking a heavy toll. In the last days, its remaining planes were totally grounded for lack of fuel. By this time, the Navy had gotten used to going it alone.

1   German cruisers at sea in the Baltic, 1944–1945. Photograph courtesy of the Imperial War Museum, London.

2 *Deutschland/Lützow*—armored cruiser. Photograph courtesy of the Naval School, Mürwik.

3 *Prinz Eugen*—heavy cruiser. Photograph courtesy of the Naval School, Mürwik.

4 *Schlesien* (old battleship) foundering but still firing at Swinemünde. Photograph courtesy of the Imperial War Museum, London.

5 *Köln* (light cruiser) flying *Reichsmarine* (pre–1935) colors. Photograph courtesy of the U.S. Naval Institute, Annapolis.

6   Z-38—destroyer. Photograph courtesy of the Naval School, Mürwik.

7 T-*Tiger* (torpedo boat) flying *Reichsmarine* colors. Photograph courtesy of the U.S. Naval Institute, Annapolis.

8 S-Boat (motor torpedo boat) with later armored bridge. Photograph
courtesy of the Naval School, Mürwik.

9 S-boat (motor torpedo boat) with later armored bridge. Photograph
courtesy of the Imperial War Museum, London.

10 R-boat (motor minesweeper) 406. Photograph courtesy of the Naval
School, Mürwik.

11 MFP (landing craft, tank) used as gun barge. Photograph courtesy of the
Naval School, Mürwik.

12 Armed trawler. Photograph courtesy of the U.S. Naval Institute, Annapolis.

13 Fish cutter—KFK. Photograph courtesy of the Naval School, Mürwik.

14 German Baltic refugee ship escorted by R-boats. Photograph courtesy of the Imperial War Museum, London.

15   Refugees assembling in marshalling area preparatory to boarding ship—Fall 1944. Photograph courtesy of the Naval School, Mürwik.

16 Troops waiting to load—Fall 1944. Photograph courtesy of the Naval School Mürwik.

5

Naval Control of Shipping

THE *HANDELSMARINE*—1939–1944

When World War II began in 1939, the *Handelsmarine* counted an apparent 4,300,000 tons of ships. It had the fifth-largest merchant fleet in the world. It was a good, efficient merchant service, carefully built up by Hitler as an accompaniment to his Navy. It was to carry quite a load, military and civil. Germany's war had to be kept going. At the same time, people had to be fed and commerce maintained, at least on a minimum basis.

In 1939 Stalin had granted the Germans use of his ice-free port of Polyarny, on the Murmansk coast, as a base. Polyarny had proven of tremendous help to merchantmen running home through the fog and ice of the far northern Atlantic during the first months of the war. Liner *Bremen* (51,731 GRT) had come that way, stopping at Polyarny for rest, repairs, and supplies before continuing south through the Norwegian leads. So opened the merchantmen's war.

Germany's war economy required a steady supply of strategic raw materials: iron ores, wolfram, petroleum, tin, bauxite, rubber, wood pulp, edible oil. The *Handelsmarine* was charged with bringing these in, through the Allied blockade when necessary. So while in 1939 and even 1940 merchantmen made the best of their own way to home ports, by 1941 supplies were arriving regularly—almost on order. By 1944, however, blockade running was over. The blockade was tighter. Sources had dried up. Polyarny was gone.

In the first years, the merchant and fishing fleets provided the essential weather reporting trawlers, the replenishment tankers, and the supply ships that, from secret rendezvous areas, supported the Navy at sea. Then in 1941, in a single two-month period, fifteen of them in the Atlantic were sunk or captured—or scuttled by their crews to prevent capture—effectively ending most of their activity there. In the Indian Ocean, they continued their work for several more years, replenishing raiders, and later, U-boats. Then they too were done.

For some time, however, the German merchant marine as a whole escaped being fully organized for total war. After all, the Nazis had only been in power for six years when the war began in 1939, and they had not yet gotten around to centralizing control over this particular sector. Many traces of even medieval practices and attitudes remained, colorful perhaps, commercially convenient, but basically not fit for modern war.

Shipping losses were, therefore, larger than they needed to be right from the first, and soon cumulatively larger than could be allowed to continue. In the first ten months of the war, the *Handelsmarine* lost 600,000 tons of ships through enemy action. Of this, 350,000 tons were seized by the Allies while attempting to run home through the blockade. Another 250,000 tons were lost during the Norwegian campaign. In the latter half of 1940, 48,000 more tons were lost.

Thereafter, the *Handelsmarine's* losses from all causes had been as follows: 1941—335,000 tons; 1942—207,000 tons; 1943—170,000 tons; 1944—349,000 tons.

During the long course of the war, the *Kriegsmarine* requisitioned about 1,000,000 tons of merchant shipping for its own purposes. These ships became transports, supply ships, tankers, training ships, accommodation ships and the like. From the fishing fleet came trawlers and drifters to function as patrol boats, minesweepers, and weather ships. In the spring of 1942, about 200,000 tons of the less suitable ships were returned to their owners.

Available merchant ships had to be shared always among civilian and military users. As losses mounted and there was little new construction, shipping became increasingly scarce. It soon had to be supplemented by chartering ships from the occupied countries. The pinch was beginning to be felt.

In 1943 a start was made on what was called the Hansa shipbuilding program. This program aimed at production of a series of three standardized hulls of the most useful sizes: 1900 tons, 3000 tons, and 5000 tons. Few of the larger sizes were in fact built, but 52 of the smallest were completed and proved a useful addition to the fleet.

KRIEGSMARINE—HANDELSMARINE

When the storm signals went up in the Ostsee, the *Kriegsmarine*, to its everlasting credit, paid full attention. Almost no matter what happened, it was certain that already scarce merchant shipping was going to play a very, very critical role. *Der Löwe* (Dönitz) was not going to get caught short. To obtain the most out of what shipping remained and was available, some effective central authority was necessary, and he was going to be it. Therein lies another interesting story.

When the war began in 1939, no real basis for naval control of shipping had yet been laid. There were no common Navy–merchant service signal books. There were no steaming diagrams for convoys and escorts. The *Kriegsmarine* used an alpha-numeric grid system to report its positions; the merchantmen used regular geographic coordinates (latitude and longitude), of course. There were no instructions concerning the blacking out of ships or camouflage painting them. The Navy did not even have a large enough supply of navigational charts to issue full relevant sets to all merchant ships needing them. (Merchant vessels usually keep to a fairly predictable route and timetable, or at least area, and rarely carry large-scale charts, tide tables, light lists, or sailing directions for other areas.) There had been no joint training involving merchant officers.

The *Kriegsmarine* could, of course, requisition and charter merchant ships, time (bareboat) or voyage. Otherwise, it could determine their cargoes and routes. It was expected to do whatever was required to protect them. But the Navy did not have full authority over them. When not involved one with the other, each went their separate ways. The merchantmen jealously guarded their position, and were practiced at it.

German merchant ship captains were no less independent than their bretheren elsewhere. They tended to live by international rules of their own. Traditionally and in maritime trading law, they were all "masters under God," and the more determined of them held that they alone were always responsible for the safety of their ship, passengers, crew, and cargo. What other allegiance they owed, they gave to their shipping lines and its owners.

Relationships between them and naval officers they worked with could be and occasionally were quite difficult. Too often the master held that he could follow naval guidance or not, as he alone saw fit. Theoretically, that left the naval officer with whom he was dealing no choice in case of serious disobedience but to shoot him. Both would be correct, as their respective worlds saw it. Liaison officers faced the problem every day. There is no record of anybody having to be shot. (These tensions are institutionalized, and have never really been solved to this day. The British Royal Navy and the Merchant Navy faced these same tensions during the Falklands War in 1982.)

EARLY COOPERATIVE EFFORTS

In 1939, *Kriegsmarinedienstellen* (KMDs)—naval service field offices—were established. Responsible for organizing the routing of naval transport and supply ships as well as commercial carriers sailing within their areas, they were more liaison officers than commanding authorities, transmitting instructions by means of conferences and consensus with individual masters. Masters could and did refer controversial matters back to their respective company offices, to be settled by other means.

KMDs had been set up in Hamburg, Bremen, Stettin, and Königsberg, and elsewhere as called for. They were opened, closed, and shuffled around as the war went on. As shortages and strains began to appear, KMDs proved insufficient for the task. Since they were administratively useful, they were never entirely closed out.

As the Germans were learning, this absence of centralized control of shipping was a luxury that could be afforded only as long as shipping was plentiful, needs were marginal, and routes were relatively safe. The duplication of routes by competing shipping lines, inefficient scheduling—especially in light of the need for convoy escort—all ate up increasingly scarce assets. The Allies were here taking a mounting toll, too. Something had to change.

In 1943, a Reich Commissioner for Shipping (Reikosee) was tried. Reikosee (Gauleiter Kaufmann in Hamburg) was charged with gaining centralized control and economic use of merchant shipping, integrating the European coastal trade and all of Germany's waterborne transport into one service. Reikosee was of course a party man, responsible directly to Hitler. His appointment caused considerable misgiving in some quarters, and in the event he proved not up to the job. Only through the sound common sense of practical men working on the spot was the system working at all.

SEETRA (SEA TRANSPORT OFFICER)

So, when the very first signs of serious trouble appeared in the Baltic, in the summer of 1944, Admiral Dönitz himself took over control of all available merchant shipping. The Navy had suggested this before, but this time the idea stuck. All merchant shipping from then on sailed when, where, and how it was told by the Navy.

Dönitz picked a good man he could trust to act for him in this matter, and gave him plenary authority to do so. Captain (almost immediately promoted Rear Admiral) Konrad Engelhardt was an energetic, experienced sea transport officer who had seen wartime service in France, Italy, Africa, the Crimea, and the Baltic. He was already in place, "wearing two hats," sitting on the *Wehrmacht* as well as the Navy staff as

Seetra. Engelhardt requisitioned what ships he needed, imposing coordination on the two sea services. Dönitz backed him to the hilt.

Working as a rule through the KMDs, Seetra (Engelhardt) was able
to accomplish wonders with only a small staff of his own. He first set
up shop in Eberswalde, on the Stettin-Berlin rail line. Forced to leave
by the Soviet advance, he moved to Hamburg. Bombed out of there, he
soon located a functioning but unseaworthy ship, had her towed to
Flensburg, and moved on board. Among other things, she had a working
marine radio. It was from *Malaga* that Seetra orchestrated the final rescue
work.

Seetra's own staff was organized into sections as follows: troop transports; refugee ships; cargo ships, hospital ships and transports for
wounded; inland shipping; fuel; administration and supply. Between
them, they were the ones who actually manged the coming Baltic lift.

Otherwise, Dönitz simply gave the already existing Baltic naval command structure naval control of shipping duties in addition to their other
duties. Admiral Kummetz at Kiel was given supervisory shipping responsibility for the entire Baltic. He and Engelhardt worked very closely
and successfully together until the end. His subordinate admirals made
things work in their areas.

Beyond stating that, however, the organizational structure here gets
a little difficult to follow. It is almost as if the right people were identified
and placed in jobs discovered to be unfilled. Since these jobs were necessary, some official cover had to be and was found for them. Operating
at the highest levels, Captain Engelhardt had suddenly become *Wehrmacht* Sea Transport Officer (Seetra-chef in the *Wehrmacht* jargon). As a
Wehrmacht staff officer, Engelhardt had authority across the several services. Naval control of shipping is a pragmatic science, at best.   •

The Navy had been employing its own transports in this work since
fall. Some 6000 Hitler Youth and 50,000 Memellanders were thus evacuated from Memel, Germany's easternmost port. By the close of 1944,
the Navy itself had brought out some 47,000 people. But even this was
nothing to what was to come. To meet that requirement, more than
naval transports and auxiliaries would be needed.

ENGELHARDT & CO.

Then-Captain Engelhardt began earmarking suitable evacuation and
supply ships in the fall of 1944. Dönitz gave him a free hand and full
support. For Engelhardt, there were two main sources for available
ships: the merchant shipping lines, which still retained many laid-up
ships; and the Navy itself, in the form of its many large liners used as
accommodation ships. Both could prove difficult to get at.

Engelhardt used the *Grossadmiral*'s authority both to overrule the objections of jealous and fearful Nazi officials, and shipowners who did not want their ships to participate in such obviously dangerous operations until they had full guarantees as to payment for any losses. Or so they said.

Even as *Götterdämmerung* approached, the Nazi party officials were reluctant to relinquish any of their authority over merchant shipping, no matter how necessary that might be. Reich Commissioner for Shipping Gauleiter Kaufmann in Hamburg, whom Engelhardt was actually supplanting, was leader of the lot. The tides of war could shift again after all. That fight Reikosee lost.

Some of the shipping lines must also have begun to think of saving something for after the war. They must have known that paper money would prove to be of little value then, but that sound ships (and coal and fuel oil) could prove to be of great use. Some must have played for time. Seetra either settled or overrode every ploy.

The U-boat training command in Danzig (one training division in Gotenhafen, one in Pillau) controlled a large number of the best remaining liners, using them for staff accommodation ships (liners or other passenger ships converted to barracks ships for military or civilian personnel—they remained moored at their berths, keeping full hotel service staff but reduced deck and engine crews) and the like. The command proved reluctant to give them up, notwithstanding the growing crowds of refugees flooding the quays. Cooperate they would not.

Engelhardt appealed to Dönitz again. Dönitz responded by offering the command to Hitler for conversion to infantry and use at the front. Hitler refused to allow this, and Dönitz ordered the U-boat training divisions to move back west to Lübeck, employing the accommodation ships to do so. After loading naval personnel, the ships were to be topped off with refugees. When the move was complete, the ships were to be turned over to Seetra.

The U-boat command complied, of course, but apparently with as little grace as they could get away with. In several instances, this attitude was to produce unfortunate results, as we shall see.

Engelhardt immediately began putting earmarked and requisitioned ships into the very best shape possible. Most of the liners had been in a care and maintenance status. Some needed repair. Some needed crews. The last stocks of oil, the last reserves of coal were located and seized, although as it proved, there was always something more to be found. Thanks to Seetra, the Navy was ready when called. As ready as it could be, at any rate.

Engelhardt & Co. were the single most important element making this greatest of all amphibious lifts a success, insofar as it was one. Seetra used up the last available ship, the last fuel to move the last possible person in the time he had to do it. He improvised. I suspect that he stretched the regulations on occasion. He may even have been less than charming, once or twice. But he got the job done. And Dönitz trusted him.

Since it was MOK Ost which carried out Seetra's orders, Engelhardt sent Kummetz a carefully selected liaison officer. Lieutenant Commander Eschricht ended up as, next after Seetra himself, probably the best informed officer on the staff. He kept track of all figures on refugees, wounded, troops waiting to be picked up, the weather conditions, and the invariably prevailing shipping bottlenecks.

Supporting Engelhardt as he mobilized the merchant service were three naval service field offices: one in Hamburg (under Vice Admiral Lohmann) with branches in Lübeck (Rear Admiral Bütow), Kiel, and Flensburg; another in Stettin (Commander Nicol) with branches in Swinemünde, Sassnitz, and Kolberg; and one in Danzig (Commander Bartels) with branches in Gotenhafen, Hela, and Pillau. Engelhardt established his own special office in Libau (Commander Harries) with a branch in Windau. These offices were staffed with former merchant service personnel, cognizant of the ways of merchant ships, commissioned in the Navy for wartime service.

The best of Engelhardt's men became troubleshooters—*missi dominici*, really—sent out with plenary powers to sort out various specific evacuation problems. Dönitz repeatedly made it clear that Engelhardt exercised full authority within his field, and the Engelhardt spoke for him. Engelhardt's troubleshooters were like most of his men, former merchant officers. They used their powers to the full. They were frequently tested, too.

In early March, Stolpmünde was about to be overrun by the enemy. Arriving in town on the sixth, one of Engelhardt's men cleared the town of 20,300 refugees in two days. The little harbor had been blocked; he reopened it, utilizing whatever labor was at hand. Tied up in port were 14 ships of between 200 and 1500 GRT; he filled them with refugees and sent them west. A small fleet of fishing trawlers, tugs, pilot boats, excursion boats, ferry-barges, motor launches, anything that floated and looked seaworthy, followed in their wake. He finished just ahead of the Red Army, leaving finally on a submarine chaser, the last boat out. For Commander Kolbe, it was all in a day's work.

In early March, some 70 ships lay in the harbor and roadstead of Swinemünde. *General San Martin* (11,251 GRT) was among them, being converted from a simple refugee ship to a transport for wounded troops. However, *San Martin* lacked sufficient oil, water, and provisions even for a minimum voyage to Danzig and then back to Copenhagen. Engelhardt's Assistant Paymaster Peter Schiller arrived on March 12, rounded up the necessary supplies, and got *San Martin* under way, despite among other things a 700-plane raid on March 14.

Not just the troubleshooters but everyone in Admiral Engelhardt's organization achieved wonders, every day. Stettin in peacetime had been a city of 400,000 people. Inevitably, it had become a transshipment point for westbound refugees. During April, under fire, Commander Nicol (officer-in-charge, Naval Service Field Office Stettin) cleaned out the city. Using every kind of small ship and craft, and with the help of some naval units, almost all the civilians, wounded, and finally the troops were removed west. Only some 7000–8000 civilians—mostly the elderly who did not want to go—were left. An entire city had been enabled to flee to the west.

In the field, the organizational structure that actually organized and ran the convoys appears to some extent just to have grown, as specific local needs were identified and met. In Danzig, Engelhardt's Commander Bartels became, in effect, Burchardi's operations officer. It was he who organized the merchant ships and crews for the convoys, and loaded them. Bartels probably knew more about the embarkation and supply of large bodies of men than any other German naval officer. He was well placed. Engelhardt did not object.

AIR THREAT

Aircraft of both Red air forces—those of the Red Air Force itself as well as those of the naval air arm—matched the advance of Russia's other arms, following closely behind. First, as the shores of the Gulf of Finland were cleared, planes moved into littoral air strips, and then swarmed over the Gulf. The same happened as the other arms carved their way to the Baltic at Lithuania and East Prussia. Soon they dominated the sea lanes, more or less at will.

Baltflot naval air arm's aircraft count hovered in this period around 700 planes, its losses constantly made good by the Western Allies. Many of these planes were twin-engined U.S.-built medium-range maritime patrol craft. These "Bostons" carried either a single torpedo or two good-sized bombs. Fighters there were, in plenty.

By day, Soviet naval aviation usually attacked targets that had previously been located by reconnaissance. Planes approached their targets closely, flying low. They then attacked in several waves, following each other closely. Composition of a typical wave: 4–6 Bostons, among them 2–3 armed with torpedoes; 4–6 fighters for flak suppression and escort.

By night, Soviet naval aviation engaged in free hunting only, without notable result.

Available too were the fighters and ground attack planes of the Red Air Force, in effectively limitless number, on which the naval air arm could call. Joint Navy–Air Force operations regularly took about four days to set up, experience taught the Germans.

The Red air forces could always marshal large numbers of aircraft for joint operations against predesignated targets. Soviet planes were thus at this point a continuing threat, especially to the ports. They were otherwise inflexible at sea, allowing many targets of opportunity to slip by. Pilots did not always press their attacks home, sheering away at the first sign of serious defense.

The almost complete absence of *Luftwaffe* fighter defense; the great number of unescorted, unarmed lone small merchantmen; the swarm of small naval ships and craft tied to generally known tasks such as minefield patrol or convoy escort; the manifold problems involved in bringing away crowds of evacuees, sometimes having to be ferried out from beaches in landing craft—all this made it easy for Soviet air.

With their excellent antiaircraft armament, larger naval vessels like cruisers and destroyers easily beat off the few air attacks made on them, the ships they might be escorting, and the ports they were helping defend.

By May 1945, destroyer Z–34's armament included no less than five dual purpose 5-inch guns, four 37-mm, and 16 20-mm, light automatic antiaircraft guns. Armored shields for the light antiaircraft guns had proven their worth, and were being mounted. There was seldom any shortage of targets at which to shoot.

Every effort to assist the merchantmen in defending themselves was made, whether in convoy or not, under escort or not. The Navy itself provided light AA guns and crews for these ships, regularly.

In the more dangerous areas, especially for ships sailing in convoy, communications teams and carefully trained naval liaison officers were placed on board. As time went on, seagoing light naval AA teams were stationed in port just outside those areas. They would make a run with a merchantman going one way, offload on the other end, and return with yet another ship.

The imperatives of an increasingly evident mass civilian evacuation had an inevitable impact on air operations. Soviet planes achieved major results from strikes during the evacuation of Memel (January 27, 1945), Danzig and Gotenhafen (end of March), Königsberg and Pillau (April 25), and Kolberg (mid-April). The dense concentration of targets and a tendency on the part of some to panic undoubtedly aided the enemy in this.

Altogether, though, only a probable 40 merchant types (134,000 tons) and 27 small naval craft were lost to air attack *at sea*. During the last six months, only 15 ships of any real size were lost, all merchantmen.

SUBMARINE THREAT

Fortunately, the Red Air Force was heavily involved in land-oriented operations. The naval air arm concentrated on the ports. Neither really had much time for scattered targets at sea. That left submarines, mines, and the surface threat, coming now out of Turku and Hangö as well as Kronstadt. We shall take the submarines first.

The submarine threat was slow to materialize. Soviet Baltic submarine commanders in general lacked experience of combat. Their boats—obsolescent designs to begin with—had lain idle at Kronstadt for two years. Their torpedoes were inferior, exploding prematurely or not at all, and running wild. Their hydrophones were crude devices. Their engines were noisy. And their crews were short of experienced enlisted men, withdrawn to fight as infantry in the desperate battles ashore. But they would learn and make the most of what they had.

Considerable thought and effort was expended on Baltflot submarines. When scheduled to pass through an enemy minefield submarines were given a thick coat of insulating paint, probably as protection against hydroelectric mines. In addition, temporary wooden frames were mounted in such a way as to prevent fouling mines with horizontal rudders, bilge keels, or other projections from the hull.

Passages were energetically supported by light forces and from the air.

In the autumn of 1944, when Soviet submarine operations in the Baltic proper first again became possible, a concerned SKL estimated that the Russians could muster some 20 combat-ready boats. In October these submarines reopened the action by sinking several small vessels off the nearby coasts of Kurland and East Prussia. As German traffic moved south and west to Danzig, West Prussia, and beyond, so did the enemy boats, hunting targets and laying mines.

No Soviet commander willingly came very close to shore; there, the water was too shallow for diving and they were too easily seen. Except to lay their mines, they hung off to the west or north of natural traffic choke points like Stolpe Bank, west of Danzig. They used their mines to force German traffic out of the swept channels inshore into the deeper water where they waited, as well as to complicate escort. As enemy traffic passed, offshore now, waiting Red submarines would attack it with torpedo and deck gun. Here, too, submarines tended to operate under the cover of darkness, during the long nights.

Soviet submarines not infrequently attacked Swedish merchantmen. At first Swedish ships steamed singly, according to normal peacetime practice. Stockholm soon was forced to introduce compulsory convoys for its ships, and to escort them. Swedish escorts did not hesitate to depth charge hostile contacts.

Submarines could be built and repaired in Baltflot's Leningrad yards. Minor work could be done at Kronstadt. Submarines could also be barged in from the White Sea during the ice-free season via Russia's inland waterways, either in disassembled form or—if small enough—operationally almost ready. There was no shortage of them.

Once developed, the submarine threat remained a very substantial one right to war's end. Nonetheless, while indeed sometimes spectacular, their actual successes turned out to be few in number.

MINE THREAT

Mines were a weapon the Russians knew from earlier wars and freely used, offensively and defensively. They were dropped from the air, laid from submarines, and kicked off surface craft, all in astronomical numbers. By 1945 there were several hundreds of thousands of them in the Baltic, although not all Russian, of course.

The great Russian tradition has been in the field of mines, and they had developed good ones. They had a moored mine with antennas, a magnetic bottom mine, a moored mine inertial firing device. The Soviets even had an anti-sweep device, one which cut the sweep cable.

Mines are of two general kinds: moored and bottom. Being limited by the weight of its mooring cable, the contact-activated moored mine can be used only in depths of up to about 200 fathoms (1200 feet). The ground mine—magnetic, acoustic, or pressure—is effective only in depths up to about 25 fathoms (or 150 feet). The Germans had to be prepared to deal with all of them.

The numerous minefields laid earlier by the *Kriegsmarine* in the Gulf of Finland, the Gulf of Riga, and elsewhere caused the Red Fleet much trouble. But mines were a two-edged sword, and German minesweepers were always hard put to keep their repeatedly and heavily mined shipping lanes clear.

Minesweeping was a tedious, slow, and expensive business. Any minefield not actively defended could be swept. Anti-sweeping devices only slowed the process—they did not prevent it. In any field, mine types could be mixed; this tended to make sweeping harder but also did not stop it.

On August 18 in the process of thickening and extending an existing German minefield, the 3rd Torpedo Boat Flotilla ran itself into a field in waters that were supposedly safe. As a result, three of the torpedo boats were lost.

On December 12, destroyers Z–35 and Z–36 were lost while in the process of thickening minefields in the western Gulf of Finland. The circumstances were similar.

One could, however, never be sure that the Russians had not quietly managed to extend known German fields or to close swept German paths, without them knowing it. Mine warfare was never simply a straightforward matter of laying fields. It was always a matter of move and scheme, plot and countermove, with surprise always playing an important operational role.

In any event, mines were a never-ending threat. Paths had to be cleared through existing fields, and continually check-swept. Paths cleared by the enemy had to be closed and traps had to be prepared.

SURFACE THREAT

The surface threat to Seetra's operations from Baltflot now should have been considerable. But Russia's heavy ships did not dare to try conclusions at sea. Mostly obsolescent, unused for two years except as floating artillery, giving gunfire support to the army defending Leningrad, with many experienced men little by little drafted to fight ashore, they would have been no match for the tough, battle-worthy, hardened *Kriegsmarine*. Moscow had evidently made a quite conscious decision to conserve what remained of their surface fleet, else little of what follows is likely to have taken place.

Since, then, the Soviets were still not committing anything destroyer-sized or larger to the fight, the surface threat came instead almost entirely from 78 or more motor torpedo boats (read torpedo cutters), some 300 minesweepers of various sizes and types, and the wide miscellany of motor gunboats and other smaller inshore craft. There were even armored motor gunboats, with tank guns.

The bulk of the Soviet torpedo cutters—the most direct surface threat—were by any standard light boats, developed from, and in many ways still resembling, British Thornycroft boats from World War I, once used against them. These 16-ton, 63-foot cutters had hydroplane hulls. They were gasoline-powered, and very fast. They carried two torpedoes (stern-launched), one light automatic gun, one searchlight, and one "smoke box." They could and did occasionally carry a few (four) mines, or raiding parties.

The torpedo cutters were no match for the heavier S-boats, but there were at the very least 78 of the cutters, and they were regularly supported by minesweepers and motor gunboats. They were also being steadily reinforced by larger U.S.- and British-built boats being brought in from Murmansk and Archangel via inland waterways. So while one-on-one contact with the S-boats was avoided, whenever German defenses could be saturated, they were.

Torpedo cutters were used offensively against German convoys, individual patrol boats, and bombardment units, and to lay scattered mines. They were used defensively, to help guard their minefields in the eastern Gulf. They continually shadowed enemy units. At night, the distant roar of their engines was a common sound.

Sometimes, massed, they fought with courage and often their tactics were good. In other cases, they showed themselves inadequately trained, nothing but a disorderly mob, burning their stern lights during a fight, getting into each other's way. They frequently attacked in conjunction with planes, something the Germans did not do.

The torpedo cutters had led the two-year guerrilla war fought in the eastern Gulf. Even before the mines and nets barring the way into the Baltic proper were removed, these boats were feeling their way through them, or were being led around them by Finnish pilots. They were pushed forward aggressively, keeping rough pace with the advance of Soviet arms ashore. The cutters used Memel and Cranz as advanced bases immediately they were taken. They were working out of Neufahrwasser (just outside—north of—Danzig) even before the *Wehrmacht* had been fully cleared out of the area.

These cutters did, however, relatively little damage against properly defended targets. In all, they sank only T–31, M-37 freighter *Neuwerk* (804 GRT), and damaged one destroyer and one 2500-ton cargo ship. What they did do was add continually to the great strain already placed on tired German crews.

GERMAN ASW

German antisubmarine (ASW) measures have been criticized by much better experts than the author. The Baltic was for so many past years a German lake, safe enough to become home to the Fleet Training Squadron and to the submarine training command, that the *Kriegsmarine* undoubtedly had trouble shifting its attitude when the situation changed. But there was more to it than that.

Until the fall of 1944, the Gulf of Finland's mine and net barriers had worked. Indeed Soviet submarines had occasionally been seen between the barriers in the Gulf, and until the net was laid, a few submarines did succeed in breaking through into the Baltic proper. But the net finally brought this to a stop. Until the barrier patrols were driven off and paths were cut through or cleared around the barriers, no more enemy submarines ever reached the Baltic.

Little more was necessary. German convoys at this point generally consisted of two or three freighters and tankers escorted by two to four trawlers or R-boats, poorly armed and inadequately equipped for ASW. As much as possible, these convoys utilized passages between the many islands immediately off the cost.

By this time, the Germans knew about both radar and sonar. For ASW they used versions of both as well as depth charges. But small escorts carried only hydrophones, and S-boats not even that. They never became expert at submarine detection, location, and attack as did, say, the Royal Navy. Even the 9th and 10th Escort Divisions were not formed until the summer and fall of 1944, and hardly had time to find themselves before the crisis.

Although the Kurland beachhead support operations continued to put a great strain on German escort forces, the Navy even in 1944 had managed to bring out a creditable number of both military wounded and refugees. In November they shepherded 704 vessels totalling 1,600,000 tons across the Baltic without a single loss. In December, as things heated up, the figures were 575 ships totalling 1,100,000 tons; in this, they lost only one trawler. After the New Year, figures get progressively hazy, but the work went on. Soon it was only a swirling nightmare, worsening day by day.

The best explanation to all this would seem to be that German losses to submarine attack—coldly calculated and serious as they were—continued to be bearable, considering the overall situation. Proper convoy escort and defense against submarine required a tremendous number of resources: surface escorts, aircraft, manpower, staffs. The *Luftwaffe* never developed an airborne ASW capability. By 1944, the other resources could either not be found or no longer existed.

Prodigies of convoy organization and control were demanded, and the demand was met as best the Navy could. Transports and refugee ships competed with the big cruisers for what escorts there were. There were never enough. For this, everyone paid. Yet a quite extraordinary operational structure made the utmost out of what there was. Soon anything with a gun became an escort.

6

The *Handelsmarine*

SITUATION IN JANAURY '45

In preparing for what quite evidently had to be a long drawn-out enterprise of tremendous proportions—so much had to be clear by then—the entire available merchant marine and fishing fleet was in due course to be mobilized. Ships of all sorts and sizes were assembled, among them the pride of the great German shipping lines. The roster was a long one.

Included were *Cap Arcona* (27,564 tons), *Robert Ley* (27,288), *Wilhelm Gustloff* (25,484), *Hansa* (23,130), *Hamburg* (22,117), *Deutschland* (21,046), and eight other liners of over 10,000 tons. Another 25 large cargo ships were also to participate in the coming ferry runs to the west. So also were many other vessels too numerous to be counted, some too insignificant to be known, including local watercraft.

As the Red Army drove toward Berlin, refugees tended to be shunted aside, forced inexorably toward the sea. It was just as well. Land transport sufficient to cope with such a tremendous mass of humanity just did not exist. Roads and railroads were in any case constantly being cut by the enemy.

There was thus only one practicable remaining large-scale escape route—by sea. While the refugees gathered in the ports and on the beaches waiting for transport, the Navy established soup kitchens in harbor sheds or in makeshift shelters. The scenes of human misery and

Table 6.1
Lift of Refugees from the East, January to May 1945

From Danzig, Gotenhafen, Hela (January/May)

    1,047,000 civilian refugees

    300,000 troops (including wounded)

From Libau (January/May)

    75,000 wounded

    25,000 other troops

From Königsberg and Pillau (January 25/April 25)

    451,000 civilian refugees

    141,000 troops (including wounded)

From Kolberg (mid-March)

    70,000 civilian refugees

    7,500 troops (including wounded)

Source: These numbers are from Mallmann-Showell. The total here is 2,116,500 people. This is necessarily an incomplete figure. In many cases there were only partial manifests or, especially in the closing days, no manifests at all. There were also other lifts, at other places, some before the turn of the year.

terrible desperation cannot even now be described. Armed sentries soon had to be posted on ships' gangways, checking boarding passes. Yet in the midst of all this agony there was hope—the ships.

For the merchant ships, Pillau and Danzig were to prove the big staging areas. Beginning as early as July, from Reval and Riga, Windau and Libau, the evacuees—eventually 500,000 would be brought down from there—were routinely carried south in smaller coasters. At Pillau and Danzig they were then transshipped onto larger ships for further movement west, along with those collected directly at the staging areas.

Merchant traffic soon learned that Soviet air attack could be avoided by sailing at night. That became routine.

It was at this point that Admiral Engelhardt released those 14 large liners for service. There came in addition those 25 freighters as well as many other smaller ships. They arrived not one moment too soon. Refugee backlogs were building up faster than they could be moved in every port. Even without Russian interference, the task was going to be enormous. And, the Soviets were going to make the job as difficult as they could. (See Table 6.1.)

WILHELM GUSTLOFF

For those ships engaged in the evacuation from the Danzig area, the former cruise liner *Wilhelm Gustloff*'s sailing was typical. Even as early as January, departures were becoming chaotic. *Gustloff* had been employed as an accommodation ship by the submarine training detachment. When the submarine command decided to move her and some other ships west, the seaman and engineering departments had to be rebuilt almost from scratch. A pick-up mixed Navy and merchant crew ws accordingly collected from around the area.

Gustloff was technically a naval transport. When she left she carried among her passengers a number of submarine service trainees. She was also being used as a hospital ship, although she bore no markings as such, and no international notice had been made. But by far the largest number of those carried were evacuees. She was armed. And she was sailed independently, by the submarine command, without adequate escort, on January 30.

This was winter in the Baltic, remember. That night was, as might be expected, a bitterly cold one. *Gustloff*—in the far-off days of peace designed to carry only 1465 passengers and a crew of 400—crammed an estimated 8000 passengers on board this night. As she pushed west through a stiff chop, ice formed on her decks. Flurries of snow obscured a fitful moon. Her lookouts were numb with cold, but in any case could see little beyond the ship. In wartime, this was a recipe for disaster.

At 302108 Jan, a spread of three torpedoes fired by Russia's S–13 (Captain Third Class Alexander Marinesko) struck *Gustloff*, and she began to sink. The scratch crew mostly did their best, but proved unequal to their task. Counting those who died as the ship went down together with those who perished later, it is probable that some 6000 persons lost their lives. The death toll here was five times as great as that on *Titanic*, and more than twice that on *Titanic* and *Lusitania* put together.

Torpedo boat T–36 (Lieutenant Robert Hering), which had been escorting *Admiral Hipper* west, quickly arrived on the scene. In spite of reports of submarine activity nearby, T–36 joined the rescue effort. Sonar picked up an echo 1400 yards away. Hering swung his ship so as to keep his bows toward the echo, and kept on working.

When the submarine approched within 1000 yards, Hering decided that he would have to move on. As torpedoes passed down either side of his ship, and sonar picked up a submarine under her stern, so quickly did T–36 pick up speed that she lost some of her own crew, swept off the nets. Depth charges were dropped to discourage the enemy as she left. But T–36 had picked up 550 people, adding them to the 250 refugees already on board (*T-Löwe*—one of the escorts—also picked up 450 people). Hering had done well.

BERLIN

Aircraft and submarines could be discriminate in their choice of targets. Mines could not. On January 31, during the evening, hospital ship *Berlin* (15,286 GRT), empty, was preparing to join a convoy out of Swinemünde, headed east. Because of ice conditions, the convoy was having difficulty forming. An icebreaker and a tug had been ordered, and were standing by. On her way out of the harbor, *Berlin* ran over a mine, holing herself in the engine and fire rooms. As the tug attempted to tow her to shallow water, where she could be beached, *Berlin* triggered another mine, and this time grounded fast. When the weather began to make up, the ship had to be abandoned where she was. Although only one man was killed, another ship was gone. So it went.

(Shipping losses for January had been bad. By no means all of them have been mentioned here. To have done so would have lost the reader in a mass of names and numbers, to little purpose. Enough has been shown to give a sufficient feel for what was going on. Things were only going to get worse. We shall continue indicating specific ships when they are of particular interest.)

FUEL

In January, too, Allied attacks on German fuel supplies were beginning to show results. Fuel was becoming an increasingly serious problem. This was especially true of coal. There was by then only a three weeks' supply of coal available for Baltic military sea transport tasks, that is, supplying Army Group Kurland. Forty thousand tons of coal en route to Norway by sea were turned around and brought back. Oil fuel was somewhat more plentiful, and oil-burning vessels were utilized where they could be had. As a rule, ships ran to and from the east until their on-board fuel was gone, upon which they were laid up for good.

Dönitz issued orders that *Emden*, whose refit had finally been abandoned, be brought back for temporary duty, and that she be used for the evacuation of refugees as soon as sufficiently ready. As other naval vessels became available for Baltic duty, they were also to be used for this purpose. These naval vessels were all oil-fueled, of course.

Under no circumstances, however, was the refugee lift to interfere with military operations. Transport of troops and supplies and the escort services rightly had to come first. If the military was allowed to come apart for lack of fuel, so did the civilian lift no matter what the stocks of fuel.

Obviously, this fuel shortage was eventually going cripple an already tight shipping situation. Effects were not immediately apparent, since most ships sailed at first with sufficient bunkers. Demands for cargo space could at this point ordinarily still be met. But as time went on and more and more merchantmen required replenishment of empty bunkers, the shortage began to be felt. When fuel ran out, the lift was over.

In February Admiral Burchardi and Commander Bartels moved north across Danzig Bay to the long narrow peninsula of Hela. Danzig itself had become untenable. Hela became the center of the evacuation effort.

COPENHAGEN—PORT OF REFUGE

Those from the east whose ships successfully ran the gauntlet of Soviet (and Allied) bombs, rockets, guns, torpedoes, and mines; those who had perhaps survived transshipment at Pillau or Danzig; were at first landed in a variety of "secure" north German ports—Swinemünde and Stettin, Lübeck and Kiel.

So many refugees had by now already been brought out that German port cities were being stuffed with them. Major efforts were being made to redistribute these people out into the surrounding countryside, but even there there were limits to what could be absorbed. The process was in any case a slow one.

Off Warnemünde, Swinemünde, and Sassnitz now lay growing numbers of ships, backed up, unable to off-load their human cargoes either there or farther west because there was no longer any place in Germany to put them. Once again, the problem could only get worse as the Red Army pushed west to their south and behind them, compressing further the still available space.

Dönitz thus now had a monster on his hands, a logistic monster called refugees. What was demanded now was some new large, secure port within reach of the big refugee ships, where they could off-load, where the evacuees could be fed and sheltered, and from which the refugees would not again immediately have to be moved. To this problem, the only possible solution was Copenhagen, in German-occupied Denmark. Both Allies were leaving Denmark alone, for reasons of their own. Copenhagen it was.

For Engelhardt, Copenhagen brought its own problems. Any port in Denmark was a longer distance from, say, Danzig than any German port. This meant that more time and fuel would be taken by each voyage. Aside from the greater shipboard logistic problems this created, additional ships would be needed and would somehow have to be found.

But there was no longer any real choice. Even Kiel—not a large city, in any case—was full, and certainly no longer safe. Bombing there was continuous, as the Allies went after its shipyards and the naval base. As the German collapse accelerated, refugees were sent north.

Dönitz's Baltic transports slogged doggedly on. They loaded refugees and wounded at Pillau, Danzig, Gotenhafen, Hela, and Kolberg as they had done all along the coast ahead of the Russians, in the face of intense efforts to stop them. Heavy casualties were inevitable, but the determined lift to the west went on.

In February, another half a million people were brought out to the west. Some three-quarters were noncombatants, the remainder wounded. For every thousand lifted out, however, another 3000 poured into the port areas. The rampaging Soviet armies could not be held. There was no longer any end.

At the end of February, the makeshift Pomeranian front collapsed, in its turn. The pocket around Danzig held out for four more weeks. A smaller beachhead was formed at Kolberg, as the Red Army came on.

GENERAL VON STEUBEN

A second German liner packed with human cargo had been sunk in February by Captain Marinesko, soon after *Gustloff*. This time it was *General von Steuben*, a 14,660-ton former trans-Atlantic liner being employed as a transport. *Von Steuben* departed Pillau early on the morning of February ninth. With normal accommodations for 500 passengers, this time she was carrying a conservative 3500 refugees and wounded. At 100053 Feb Marinesko's S–13 put two torpedoes into her. It is estimated that only some 300 reached safety, refugees mostly. The wounded could not have had any chance at all. *Von Steuben*—like *Gustloff*—had been independently sailed, by the submariners, with inadequate escort.

In late February and early March the Navy provided fire support to the hedgehog opposite Wollin. *Admiral Scheer*, three destroyers, and a torpedo boat (T–36, again) managed this task.

Two destroyers and another torpedo boat supported the 3000 troops still holding the tiny village of Kahlberg, sitting on the Frische Nehrung's barrier spit.

Hela was being built up as a refugee transshipment center. Newly arrived evacuees were off-loaded there to await further movement west. Refugees were collected from around the bay using whatever small craft could be found. Soviet guns shelled the beaches, ground attack planes bombed and strafed, tearing great holes in the waiting ranks. The big ships were met offshore by lighters full to their marks with evacuees, loaded, and moved out at once. The Hela center steadily grew, more and more the best of the available places at which to organize those still headed for safety.

By mid-March, MFP flotillas, covered by the big ships, managed to rescue some 75,000 isolated refugees from the Frische Nehrung's barrier spit, temporarily at least clearing it.

Already, transports and merchantmen were all having to lay off out in the bay. With Danzig area quays and other port facilities battered

Table 6.2
Key Merchant Ships Engaged in Lift

Name	Tonnage (GRT)	Trips	Lift (people)*
Deutschland	21,046	7	69,379
Eberhard Essberger	5,064	12	66,550
Potsdam	17,528	7	53,891
General San Martin	11,352	13	35,111
Pretoria	16,662	8	35,044
Der Deutsche	11,430	6	34,474
Lappland	7,644	6	34,233
Hestia	2,883	14	32,806
Urundi	5,791	7	32,716
Neidenfels	7,838	5	30,100
Ubena	9,554	7	27,170
Cap Arcona	27,564	3	25,795
Hamburg	22,117	3	23,057
Herkules	2,369	9	21,500
Goya	5,230	4	19,785
Södenhamn	1,499	9	19,350
Nautik	1,127	20	18,413
Karoline	887	10	6,518

*These figures may include data from the administrative 40,000-evacuee lift from Finland in 1944.

beyond use and continually under enemy fire, all small craft became tenders, shuttling between shore and whatever ships there were.

Once clear of the aircraft and artillery pounding Danzig, German shipping had still to run the gauntlet of submarines and mines found in increasing numbers along the Pomeranian coast. Commander Heydel's 10th Escort division had responsibility for this area, and he got the ships through with surprisingly few losses, despite *Gustloff* and *Steuben*.

By mid-March, the already overwhelming tide of refugees increased yet again. The Nazi party had been telling people to remain in their homes, that they would be defended. Many therefore waited too long to flee. They now mobbed the coastal areas. As the remaining ports were one by one blocked or wrecked, people found no way out.

In March, the reasons not clear, Vice Admiral Lange was relieved by Rear Admiral Schubert as Admiral, Western Baltic. Schubert remained until driven out by the enemy.

By March, too, the people's latent dislike of the party fanatics began more quickly to show itself. Dead with fatigue, the Navy's tempers were short, in any event.

In one recorded case, in Danzig Bay, torpedo boat T–28—commanded by Lieutenant Hans Temming—noticed a small steamer under way north, decks empty. T–28 hailed the steamer, asking where she was headed, and if she had any refugees on board. The steamer responded that she had Gauleiter Forster on board and was under way for Hela. T–28, awash with refugees, then requested that the steamer heave to and take some of them aboard her. The steamer failed to answer to this. T–28 then coldly announced that if the steamer did not stop, the T-boat would sink her. T–28's crew began to clear a gun. Whereupon the little steamer hove to and took off a full load, continuing to Hela. The Gauleiter was not again seen or heard from.

APRIL

By mid-April, the Russians had advanced far into Pomerania. Königsberg, Pillau, Gotenhafen, Danzig were gone. There was no longer a safe port; there were only the sand dunes of the Hela Peninsula and a few hedgehogs along the coast left. Soviet fighters and bombers strafed the dunes, their artillery pounded the beaches. With their backs to the sea the refugees waited for landing craft and small boats to ferry them out to the bigger ships (which could not come inshore). Losses among light craft could no longer even be counted. Wrecks lined the length of the coast.

Gotenhafen had been evacuated the night of April fifth. The Navy moved some 30,000 refugees and 8000 troops from Gotenhafen to Hela, in an aptly named operation *"Walpurgisnacht"*.

As the situation daily became more desperate, babies came to assume the role of tickets to safety. Parents with babes in arms often received priority for whatever shipping space was available. In some cases, infants were carried on board, then passed back ashore to relatives for re-use. In other, cases, near the end, babies were stolen from their parents and used. When all other hope seemed gone, babies were simply thrown aboard, parents hoping that someone at least would be able to care for them. Often the infants fell between the ships and the pier or quay and drowned.

The Navy responded with a combination of desperation, organization, improvisation, loyalty, and heroism. It scraped together other liners as well as tiny old freighters fit only for the breaker's yard, and shuttled them backward and forward along the Kurland, Pomerania, and Mecklenburg coast. They were under constant attack now, but always re-

The Danzig Bay Area

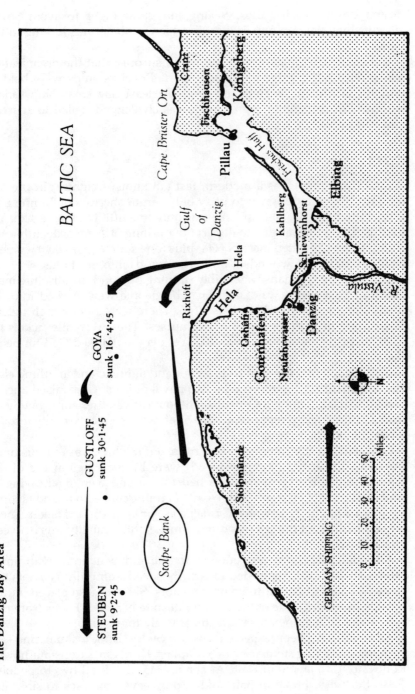

turned despite their losses. Sailing mostly at night to avoid Soviet aircraft, they were in any case vulnerable to submarines lurking in the dark.

Under the circumstances, it can be no surprise that the organization was often on the verge of coming apart. Priceless ships were held in port for lack of oil, water, and food. At least one small ship sailing without her recognition signal book was challenged, failed to answer, and was sunk.

GOYA

Goya (5230 tons) was a modern, fast (18 knots) freighter. In the far-off days of peace designed to carry only cargo, she was not a fine passenger liner like *Gustloff*, and she was only one-fifth the liner's size. Yet for this trip—she was due to depart the evening of April sixteenth—she crammed an estimated mass of 6000-plus (one source says 7000) women, children, old men, wounded, and even troops into her holds.

Time for the Germans was visibly running out, and the absolute maximum of passengers was taken on. The people were packed into the holds shoulder to shoulder, like cargo. There were not enough toilets. There were no doctors and only two nurses. There were life jackets for 3500, lifeboats and rafts for 300–400. Yet people thanked God for being there.

Goya loaded off Hela-Süd from ferries and lighters, and anything else. Her merchant staff reinforced by two naval officers, *Goya* raised anchor just after 1900, joining a Copenhagen-bound five-other-ship convoy. A meager two-minesweeper escort provided what convoy security it could (even they carried refugees).

Goya had already completed four runs, but her luck was out this time. Russian submarines (scenting blood) were by then well aware of the cleared routes the German ships had to use and were again lying in wait. Just west of Hela, off Stolpe Bank (a traffic choke point and favorite submarine haunt, near which *Gustloff* was sunk), night had fallen. There was no moon, but the sea was calm, winds light. Visibility was between one and two miles.

Although *Goya* was fast enough to sail independently with some safety, she was this night tied to convoy speed—officially 11 knots but actually, this turned out to be only 9 knots. She was also placed on the outside (northern) side of the convoy, despite her load. It was from this side that a submarine attack was most likely to develop.

As could have been expected, just off Stolpe Bank a submarine—an ancient minelaying submarine L–3 (Captain Third Class Konstantinovich Konovalov) was lying in wait. At about 2345, L–3 fired two torpedoes. *Goya*, hit twice, broke in half, taking only seven minutes to sink. On the order of 100 souls were rescued, perhaps a few more.

Improvisation was everywhere the rule now. Ships were manned with whatever naval and merchant marine officers could be found. Ships that had not moved for four years were crewed, brought to life, and sailed for the east. Many members of the crews were non-Germans. Fewer were trained seamen. There were plenty of the seemingly inevitable organizational conflicts, as well as personnel ones. For some, this improvisation did not work. But the bottom line is—for most it did.

Soviet tanks and infantry were sweeping along Germany's north coast, driving into the sea the broken fragments of the *Wehrmacht*. Here and there, at isolated bays and harbors, a few battalions of troops might be rescued by ship, a few hundreds of refugees might be saved. Parties of engineers might be landed to complete vitally important demolitions ahead of the advancing enemy. Reconnaissance parties might be landed to collect intelligence. The sea services were kept desperately busy.

Festung Kurland remained a major drain on available shipping resources. Everyone must have known it was going to represent the largest single failure. There were still 200,000 plus troops holding the pocket. No one knows how may refugees. Every ship bringing in supplies loaded refugees and troops out. Nothing more could be done.

Six months earlier, an organized evacuation of the pocket—lifting out personnel *and* equipment—was estimated to require five months. Personnel alone could have been evacuated in five weeks. That moment had been allowed to pass. It was now too late.

Both Libau and Windau were now battered beyond large-scale use, and under constant attack from the air. Windau had never been capable of handling much, anyway. That left only the open beaches, and they could not add much.

All surplus shipping seems to have been directed now to Hela. Such as there was. Fuel and time were both running out. More could still be accomplished—the runs were shorter—lifting from ports closer in.

Shipping to and from Kurland was now bypassing Hela. Hela had its own troubles, and could not now normally transship as it once had.

THE WESTERN ALLIES

By now, the most dangerous threat to the whole Baltic enterprise came not from the Red Fleet or Air Force, but from the Western Allies, especially the British Royal Air Force's bombers and fighters. RAF Bomber Command's long-range aircraft were now steadily laying mines in the western Baltic. Coastal Command's strike wings were constantly sweeping the German coast for shipping, and reaching out as far as the Kattegat.

Aircraft-laid influence mines provided air power for the first time with a weapon that permitted it to impose a continuous blockade. In January, the RAF had dropped roughly 670 mines into the Baltic shipping lanes; the very next month it laid maybe 1350 mines. The totals kept increasing, and the effect was cumulative. In the Baltic, the RAF concentrated on the waters around Swinemünde, but its planes operated as far east as the coast of Pomerania.

For instance, between January and May, Soviet submarines sank a total of perhaps ten merchantmen/transports aggregating 60,000 tons by torpedoes, three merchant types of 4000 tons and four naval vessels by mines. By contrast, in just the first three months of the year, in the Western Baltic, RAF mines sank maybe 20 ships aggregating 100,000 tons. Many more vessels were damaged but not sunk. If nothing else, these mines caused long delays while the mines were swept.

During the last few days, the United States also joined in the Allied mining effort. It was the final straw.

By now, the intensity of Allied mine laying and the constant strafing attacks were threatening to bring about a complete collapse of the German mine-sweeping service. The sweepers had so far done extremely well, but now harbors and swept channels had frequently to be closed, or were kept open only through the most extreme efforts. Both sweepers and crews were running down.

Soviet motor torpedo boats began operating from Neufahrwasser, near Danzig, in early April. Destroyer Z–34 was severely damaged by a torpedo cutter on April fifteenth, below Hela. She was brought under protection of the land, and the following day towed back to Swinemünde. She had been the last sizable naval fighting ship working in Danzig Bay, leaving the field to reserve and auxiliary units: fish cutters, ferry-barges, armed trawlers and the like. Torpedo cutters were still the largest Soviet surface vessels to intervene in the almost continuous fracas.

Despite all this, Hela was kept busy. During April, some 265,000 people were picked up from around Danzig Bay and brought to the staging area. During that same month an estimated 400,000 old men, women, children, wounded, and troops were loaded out and carried to safety in the western Baltic. This, in spite of everything the Allies were able to do.

Obviously, many merchantmen (1080) were engaged in the lift at one time or another. It is important to note that only 245 (relatively few) were lost. *Wilhelm Gustloff, General von Steuben,* and *Goya* were all three exceptional cases, unusual losses even among the larger ships. *Goya* had in fact already completed four successful round-trips, bringing out a total of almost 20,000 people. *Gustloff* was of course on her first. *Goya* was not even a liner. (See Table 6.3.)

The *Gustloff/von Steuben/Goya* casualties were also exceptional. They alone furnished almost half of all such losses—15,200 lives. (These deaths

Table 6.3
Losses at Sea during Lift from the East

Date (1945)	Name of Ship	Tonnage (GRT)	Lost/Saved
Jan 30/31	Wilhelm Gustloff	25,484	4-6,000/900
Feb 9/10	General von Steuben	14,660	3,200/300
Feb 17	Eifel	1,429	680/ ?
Mar 12	Andross	3,000	550/2,000
Apr 9	Albert Jensen	5,500	no refugees
Apr 10	Neuwerk	803	800/ ?
Apr 11	Moltkefels	7,862	1,000/3,500
Apr 11	Posen	1,062	?
Apr 13	Karlsruhe	897	800/150
Apr 16/17	Goya	5,230	6,000/100 ?
Apr 25	Emily Sauber	2,475	50/2,000

were the result of legitimate acts of war. All three ships were armed and carried troops.)

Many more did survive than did not. *General San Martin* and *Eberhard Essberger* finally tied up after making 13 and 12 trips respectively. *Deutschland* completed seven, bringing back nearly 70,000 people. *Essberger* brought out almost 67,000. (See Table 6.2.)

Little ships did more than their share. *Karoline* (887 GRT) completed ten runs, managing the amazing total of more than 6500 evacuees. *Nautik* managed a total of 20 runs. Another, *Hestia,* finished 14 of them. Small motor coasters—mostly family owned and manned—brought back perhaps another 6000 souls between them. Among those lost were *Erni* (105 GRT) and *Arkona* (all of 85 GRT).

The Allied campaign against German merchant shipping had now reached a crescendo. RAF Bomber Command's mine layers, Coastal Command's strike aircraft, Royal Navy carrier-borne aircraft and light surface forces all joined in. Together with the United States, they inflicted the final crippling losses, especially in the Skagerrak, the Kattegat, and the western Baltic. The Soviets kept up the pressure in the east.

All in all, loss patterns in the Baltic followed expectations. Bombs had accounted for the greater part of those merchant types lost (88 ships), with mines next (half as many), and torpedoes a distant third (10). (See

Appendix F.) Losses were heaviest among those ships which were inadequately escorted, or not escorted at all—or were caught in port.

By May seventh, when the Admiralty ordered all such operations to cease, normal German shipping had been brought more or less to a standstill. The lift went on. Death was already on every hand, and the Red Army every day nearer.

7

Closing Down

TWILIGHT

As May arrived, noisily, bloodily, everyone, groggy with fatigue but still on their feet fighting, the situation only looked worse, not better. There were now left only the battered remnants of armies, one still holding out in Kurland, the other in East Prussia. Each still provided safe haven for hundreds of thousands of civilian refugees. In East Prussia, the mass was being squeezed into a narrow coastal strip around the Gulf of Danzig; here, Hela was the key assembly point. None had any hope of holding out for much longer.

While the killing had definitely not stopped, to all intents and purposes the war was over. There would be no salvation of Hitler's Reich by the V–1s and V–2s, the ME–262 fighters, or the new submarines. They were too late.

Although no one used the term in those days, what was going on was "damage limitation," as we know it. Everyone was being brought out in the lift—military personnel as well as civilians. Every kind of ship—naval as well as merchant—moving east carried supplies; every one moving west carried people. Ships loaded, sailed, unloaded, loaded, sailed, shuttling back and forth as fast as they could until they broke down or until they ran out of fuel. Or they were sunk.

The crews of the German Navy's major combatants, those of the district and escort forces, as well as those of the merchantmen, numb with fatigue except when, like all others at sea, they were frightened almost out of their wits, carried on. They risked serious burns, wounds, or being drowned every hour. The sick stink of death was on every hand. The Reich was disintegrating around them. Why did they go on?

There were indeed naval police patroling behind the lines and in the ports. They summarily hung deserters. Naval courts passed sentences of death for mutiny and cowardice, and they were indeed carried out. But that cannot be the heart of the matter.

It was the operating units that held together, and they brought those with whom they had contact along with them. Shipmates depended on each other. The refugees, the wounded, sometimes even their own families, and in the final days the troops, manifestly needed them.

A half-century later, in the midst of an age which has often derided such values, this is difficult to either explain or credit. But it is a fact.

Many miles would yet be run before the final log entries were made, but as we shall see, it had not all been in vain.

SACHSENWALD

Steamer *Sachsenwald* (6261 GRT), completed only in 1945, lay off Hela on May second, riding to her anchor. She was taking on board lighter after lighter of wounded, 5500 of them, under intense artillery fire and continual air attack. She loaded all day and through the night. Early on May third, *Sachsenwald* hauled short on her anchor, fully loaded, ready to leave. As she did so, from the lighters full of refugees on either side came a terrible cry. *Sachsenwald*'s bos'n leaned over the ship's rail and called, "We will be back."

But *Sachsenwald* never was. Arriving in Copenhagen without incident, even having picked up some more evacuees along the way, she was forced to pay off. She was completely out of coal and could find no more. Copenhagen was her last port.

Sachsenwald was typical of too many ships. Clearly the rescue effort was losing momentum. If it was to continue, another round of resources was going to have to be thrown into the old pot.

As early as April thirtieth, recognizing the problem, Engelhardt had begun frantically searching for those additional ships, new stocks of oil, coal, food, and now crews still available, matching up one with the other. Not one large passenger liner, additional personnel transport, or other usable high-capacity reasonable-draft people-moving merchantman either on the Schleswig-Holstein coast or in Copenhagen remained fit for sea. Most were in any case out of fuel. There were, he found, however, a number of smaller cargo ships still to be had. These he took over, crewed, stored, fueled, and made ready as fast as could be done.

Table 7.1
Baltic Command Structure, January to May 1945

Commander-in-Chief Armed Forces	Hitler in Berlin; then
	Dönitz in Plön and Flensburg
Commander-in-Chief Navy (ObdM)	Dönitz in Berlin,
with core SKL	Wilhelmshaven, and Plön;
	von Friedeburg in Flensburg
Sea Transport Officer (Seetra)	Engelhardt in Eberswalde,
	Hamburg and Flensburg
Naval High Commander East	Kummetz in Kiel
(MOK Ost)	
Admiral Eastern Baltic	Burchardi (Thiele for last
	days) in Danzig and Hela
Admiral Western Baltic	Lange (Schubert after March)
	in Swinemünde
Battle Groups 1 (Rogge)	Controlled by MOK Ost
and 2 (Thiele)	
Escort Division 9 (von Blanc)	Under area command in Windau,
	Libau and Danzig
Escort Division 10 (Heydal)	Under area command in
	Swinemünde

On May fifth and sixth, this ragtag, nondescript, devoted fleet finally left for one last run to Hela. This time, there was really nothing left.

The *Kriegsmarine* itself contributed its share, primarily those destroyers and torpedo boats still fit. Z-boats could each load some 2000 people, the T-boats perhaps 1200 each. Good enough. Also on the fifth, four destroyers and five torpedo boats departed Copenhagen for Hela. They loaded up that night and were headed back the next day.

Sea Transport was meantime still getting calls for ships from Windau, Libau, Swinemünde, and several Mecklenburg ports, as well as Hela. It had to continue normal Kurland logistic traffic along with everything else. Seetra diverted what he could. A tremendous final effort it was. But it didn't turn out to be final.

POLITICAL COVER

OKM fought to gain for these operations what political cover it could still arrange. Depending on how one looks at it, *der Löwe* (Dönitz)—who on May first succeeded Hitler as chief of government—gained either four or eight days more time in which to bring people out to the west. The four days he gained through a local cease-fire arranged for the northwest, including Denmark, Holland, and the islands. The eight days he gained by refusing general unconditional surrender demands for as long as he dared. The last had to include *Wehrmacht* forces facing the Red Army in the east.

Dönitz's first priority had had to be to keep open as long as possible the land escape route along the Baltic coast, for those not yet caught behind the front. Even this was almost at once closed. On May second the British crossed the Elbe and, continuing east, captured Lübeck. Dönitz retreated to Flensburg.

Facing the inevitable, Dönitz promptly dispatched Admiral Hans-Georg von Friedeburg to Field Marshal Montgomery with a request for a preliminary local cease-fire, so as to be able to somehow continue the evacuation by sea. On the fifth, Montgomery finally agreed, thus giving Dönitz what turned out to be four extra days to do what he could with what was left.

Then on May seventh, Dönitz finally agreed to surrender unconditionally all remaining German armed forces. This included those still facing the Red Army in the east. The capitulation, however, would not come into force until 090100 eastern European time. The lift from the east could continue for almost two more days! That was all, though, that he could get. (See Table 7.2.)

The war, it should be remembered, was still being fought all out in the east. The Russians had had no part in the local cease-fire and would not be likely to sit idly by while the sea lift continued. The Soviets, with perhaps a greater sense of the value of skilled labor in general; with much of western Russia to rebuild; with a number of individual scores to settle; and determined to seize everything that they could as war reparations—were quite obviously going to insist that everyone and everything still in the east was theirs.

CAP ARCONA

At this point it is necessary to digress to a separate but almost certainly related issue, even though it is not one in which the Navy was directly involved. Liner *Cap Arcona* (27,564 GRT) had been the largest of the refugee ships. Built to carry 1315 passengers, she had in three trips

Table 7.2
Naval Chronology, May 1–9, 1945

May 1   Dönitz assumed the office of chief of government
            of the rump Third Reich. Von Friedeberg appointed
            new Commander-in-Chief Navy. Naval headquarters
            moved to Mürwik.

May 1/2   Von Friedeberg sent to contact British to ask for
            local cease-fire. All refugees and all wounded
            ordered evacuated into Denmark. Lift from east
            continued at frantic pace.

May 4   Montgomery's terms accepted by Dönitz.

May 5   Local cease-fire came into effect at 0800.
            Scuttling forbidden. U-boat commanders to turn
            over boats. Eisenhower declined to ratify the
            local cease-fire, demanding general unconditional
            surrender.

May 7   Dönitz agreed to surrender all remaining German
            forces, including those still facing Red Army.
            Lift from east continued with all means.

May 9   Surrender terms came into effect at 0100.
            Unofficial rescues continued for some time.

brought 26,000 people out of Danzig Bay. She had been a lucky ship, escaping several submarine ambushes during the last months. But madness still ruled the land.

By mid-April, *Cap Arcona* lay in Copenhagen. She was in bad shape, worn out through lack of maintenance and hard use. Released by the *Kriegsmarine*, she was ordered to Neustadt Bay (near Kiel) where she anchored a mile and half offshore. There she was to be paid off.

At this point, the Reich commissioner for Shipping resumed control of the ship. He ordered her to be turned into a floating prison ship, to receive the concentration camp inmates being moved from Hamburg/Neuengamme ahead of the advancing Allies. Accordingly, between

April twenty-sixth and twenty-eighth, under strong duress, *Cap Arcona* took slowly aboard 5000 detainees and their SS guards.

At 031430 May, three ships lay at anchor in Neustadt Bay: *Cap Arcona*, *Thielbek* (also carrying prisoners), and *Deutschland* (empty). They made an attractive target; the three of them were attacked by a dozen or more RAF Typhoon fighter bombers. Rocketed, bombed, and gunned, the ships had no defense. All three ships caught fire. *Cap Arcona* burned like a torch, capsized, and sank. The detainees were never released by their SS guards.

The very next day (May 4) Montgomery's troops arrived in Neustadt. When they took a tally, they counted most or all of the 5000 *Cap Arcona* prisoners as having either been burned to death or drowned. Perhaps only as many as 306 lived.

The coincidence that on the fourth the British and the Germans managed to agree to a local cease-fire (to take effect on the fifth) is too much to let pass. It would only be reasonable to assume they saw that this senseless slaughter had to be stopped. *Cap Arcona*'s luck had just run out a day too soon.

THE FINAL EFFORT

Once Greifswald, Stralsund, and Rügen Island to the west had been taken by the Red Army, Swinemünde had to fail. The oldest naval commanding officer on active duty, Vice Admiral Kreisch, had in co-operation with the Army organized the clearance of the city and port. Using five steamers, three destroyers, two torpedo boats, one AA ship, one auxiliary cruiser, and one tender, he loaded out some 35,000 people for Copenhagen. Then before leaving on May 4, the old warrior scuttled damaged old battleship *Schlesien* and armored cruiser *Lützow* in the harbor.

The writ of Dönitz's Third Reich here now only ran in a small rump area in the northwest. Only the Schleswig-Holstein peninsula, just south of Denmark, was still accessible to the refugees. There was also German-occupied Denmark, itself stuffed with refugees. British forces were taking control in both these areas, but for the moment they tended to turn a Nelsonian "blind eye" to valid evacuation activity.

It must be acknowledged that the British had adopted a much more pragmatic view of what was going on than the ever legalistic-moralistic Americans. They knew—if we did not—that in international affairs there are no permanent enemies, only permanent interests.

On Dönitz depended one final rescue effort. His *Kriegsmarine* was now all alone in this. There was no longer any air support; what little remained of the *Luftwaffe* was grounded for lack of fuel. Dönitz had little left with which to work. But he had to try, and he rose to the challenge.

between the first and eighth of May, small craft ferried 150,000 survivors into Hela alone.

A still increasing number of ships—naval and merchant—had been released for duty in the Baltic as the Reich recoiled inward upon itself. Dönitz now issued his Navy a general order, directing the use of "every ship, every cruiser, destroyer, torpedo boat, merchant ship, fishing boat and row boat"in what had to be a final evacuation effort. The charge now was, "Avoid further bloodshed; save life!"

Desperate, grim rearguards had their backs to the sea. Soviet air attacks on the remaining resistance were incessant.

Still successfully defended were the wooded sand dunes of the Hela spit, the battered ports of Kurland (Windau and Libau), and a few isolated hedgehogs scattered along the coast. That is all. The imperatives now were time (measurable in hours), space, and ships.

A pall of oily smoke, driven by an onshore wind, hung above the remaining beaches. The sharp bang of AA guns, the continuous rattle of light automatic weapons, and the boom of depth charges would too often be followed by exhausted survivors coated with oil, suffering from wounds and shock.

The naval personnel ashore and the crews of the tugs, MFPs, and other yard craft often smelled bad and looked worse—unshaven, soiled and rumpled, red of eye. But many thanked God they were still there.

The refugees—whatever they were—huddled together in shell holes, waiting at any cost for the small craft that would carry them out to the bigger ships offshore, or that would even themselves carry a load out to the west. These pockets were inevitably falling, one by one.

The *Kriegsmarine* concentrated more and more of its remaining gunships off Hela and the other beaches. These provided the antiaircraft barrages needed to keep enemy planes at a generally ineffective distance. They continued at the same time to provide gunfire support to the troops. Time could be bought for any unit with its back to the sea, within range of the ships' guns, at least for a while. Warships no longer returned to base for replenishment and rest. They replenished ammunition and fuel out in the stream, in action.

HELA

Hela was the long, thin, wooded sand spit (peninsula) which reached out 40 miles or so east from Rixhöft across the mouth of Danzig Bay. The Poles had fortified and defended it successfully for a month in 1939. The Germans, of course, took over the fortifications and in 1945 they in turn were defending it. At the peninsula's eastern tip was a fishing village of the same name which had become the center of German evacuation activity for the whole bay area. It was here more than anywhere else that the climax of this Wagnerian tragedy was acted out.

On April twenty-eighth, in Hela, for reasons not clear, Vice Admiral Thiele had relieved Admiral Burchardi as Admiral, Eastern Baltic. Thiele found some 200,000 military and civilians camped on the sand spit. He had immediately requested additional transport for them. But by April thirtieth none had come. The people waited, still.

Hela possessed two small craft harbors, one normally used as a small naval base and the other as a fishing port. Troop units and the wounded were evacuated through the naval base, civilian refugees through the other. Meanwhile, the wounded and the troops were quartered in what remained of the buildings, the civilians dug in on the dunes.

There was still something of a loose, intermittent German front in the Vistula flats, between the mouths of the Vistula and Nogat rivers and on the Frische Nehrung. The whole area was alive with small groups of refugees and with fragments of former troop units. And with the Red Army, looking for them.

Night after night, from Hela, small craft with dimmed lights stole out over the bay, searching for people to bring back. Most anywhere they approched, hundreds of people waded or were carried out to them. At several points on the Nehrung makeshift piers were built; each day they were shot up, each night they were rebuilt by those on the beach.

EXTRA DAYS

The *Kriegsmarine* made the most of its unexpected extra time. On the seventh, no other shipping being available, five more destroyers and four torpedo boats from Copenhagen (many of which had just returned from Hela), joined by two Z-boats and one T-boat from Swinemünde, made a last dash back into Hela. They loaded full in just three hours, cleared safely, and made it back to Kiel the next day. They were, unfortunately, the only ships left in the west with both the speed and fuel to manage such a run.

Squeezed by the Allies, Dönitz's political time was running out. On the seventh also, sadly, orders went out to all shipping in the Ostsee:

1. Included in the capitulation is the requirement that all major naval ships, district and escort forces and all merchant vessels clear Kurland ports and Hela by 090100 May. All ships and boats will be out-loaded to their marks, only with people. . . . Target ports are Kiel, Eckernförde and Neustadt. Danish harbors are closed.

2. Naval and merchant ships underway east which cannot load and be back at sea by 090100 will reverse course and return to Flensburg.

3. Ships en route back are to announce port and estimated time of arrival by radio.

The night of May 8–9 therefore offered what everyone concerned with the lift realized was the very last chance to escape west. The eastern and southern Baltic were witness that night to sights they may never see again.

LAST RUNS FOR HOME

The biggest evacuation was from Hela, naturally. The dark Ostsee west from Hela to Bornholm—the trunk route—was soon almost covered with ships of almost all sizes and ages and craft of all types, traveling alone and in small groups, overtaking and being overtaken. They formed yet another, this time final, larger, decidedly unmilitary single parade streaming west. The core of this parade was made up of the ships from Seetra's last convoy, but it included anything that floated; that offered protection from the sea's cold wind and wet; and that could move under its own power, or be pushed or towed. The bay was emptied. Every vessel made the best speed it could, there was no formal organization or even escort. No one really knows the numbers—record keeping was not high on anyone's list of priorities at this point—but the best estimate is that between 65 and 70 thousand people made it out that night from Hela alone.

Still further northeast, similar scenes took place. Some 175 ships and craft from Windau and Libau were organized into five (some say six) loose convoys—four from Libau and one from Windau—managing to bring out an estimated 25,300 troops. These convoys loaded and left on the evening of the eighth, literally the last minute, some of them. These were thus the evacuation's last convoys. They arrived in the west by the eleventh, all of them. Except for two straggling trawlers, that is, both of which were cut out and forced back by pursuing armed Soviet craft.

RUGARD

On the afternoon of May ninth, one of the Hela convoys was off Bornholm, still working its way in. This group of ships was being led by naval auxiliary *Rugard* (1358 tons), an old nondescript holiday steamer which was acting as headquarters ship of the 9th Escort Division. Having cleared Hela at or about 082100, *Rugard* headed a typical ragtag collection of cargo ships, tugs and barges, and assorted harbor craft, escorted by R-boats. *Rugard* herself was stuffed with refugees—several thousand of them—as were all the others, of course.

Rugard's convoy was at that point quite unexpectedly intercepted by three Soviet torpedo cutters, one of which fired across *Rugard*'s bows. These were probably part of the cutter squadron which arrived at Rönne (Bornholm) that day.

Most of the convoy now defenseless, their guns having been deliberately disabled that day, *Rugard* hove to. She did have a single old French-built 75-mm gun still able to fire. *Rugard* asked naval headquarters for orders, and was told to continue on. *Rugard*'s commander prepared to comply.

In the meantime, one of the enemy cutters pulled alongside and an officer shouted up, "Back you get! Otherwise you go to hell!" He pointed to the torpedoes and light automatic gun.

Rugard instead rang up full ahead, avoided two torpedoes, and began to receive fire. *Rugard*'s "88" opened up in reply. She soon registered a direct hit on the lead cutter, which disappeared in a cloud of smoke and steam. The two others fled. At about 2000, this, the last recorded naval battle of the Baltic, was ended. *Rugard*'s convoy made Kiel the following day, without further incident.

But the Germans' flight west did not stop here. Odd vessels like icebreakers, harbor cranes, even single motor whaleboats, some navigating only by stars and sun, others simply following the pack, kept drifting in from Hela and even far-off Libau. Seetra Libau reported himself in with his whaleboat on the thirteenth, hand to his cap.

Those said to have been officially the last arrived from Hela at 141400, after six days at sea. This unknown trawler left Hela towing a barge shortly after midnight May 8–9, bringing out a total of 135 passengers— 75 wounded, 25 women and children, and 35 troops—the skipper himself, and four hands. Food and water had been short and arrangements primitive, but everyone arrived safely.

Violent exchanges between escaping Germans and the Russians kept flaring up at sea even after the formal end of the war, as desperate people continued to be snatched by private adventurers from under Soviet guns. An unknown number were thus brought out "black." Some few were recaptured and turned back under arrest, disappearing into *Nacht* (night) and *Nebel* (mist).

8

Conclusion

END OF THE BEGINNING

By the time that Baltic operations had finally been closed down and some sort of stock could at last be taken, it was discovered that perhaps as many as 1,500,000 refugees and four Army divisions (40,000 men?) had been brought out of Kurland alone, either directly or via Danzig and Pillau. Another 900,000 had originated from Danzig and points west. Under the circumstances, this was a truly amazing feat. It had had its price, but everyone knew it would, and, considering everything, it could have been worse.

Especially in Kurland, the lack of shipping and by the end totally inadequate port facilities (battered and badly worn) meant that only a fraction of the Army could be brought out. Left behind and captured in Kurland were 42 German generals, 8038 officers, 181,032 enlisted men, and 1400 Lettish volunteers. Even in Hela, 60,000 troops had had to be abandoned. On Bornholm, 16,000 were left. The first of these took ten years to come back out of Russia. Some of the rest never made it back.

Large steamer *Moero* (6111 GRT) carrying 1273 persons (700 wounded, 573 refugees), and small steamer *Nordstern* (1127 GRT) carrying 625 evacuees, had been the first serious merchant losses in the long lift. *Moero* was attacked from the air off Reval on September twenty-second; only 618 were saved. *Nordstern* was torpedoed on October sixth off Windau; 531 died.

No one really knows the name of the last ship. Nor how many were lost with her. Like much else, this has disappeared into the murk of time. As the German clock ran down, not only was the average size of the ships involved smaller, not only did liners give way to cargo ships, not only were the evacuees jammed in under conditions that would have been unacceptable at first sight, but less and less attention could be paid to keep exact tallies.

KRIEGSMARINE

For years, in two world wars, the Baltic was considered a secondary naval theater. In 1941, *Wehrmacht* planners had failed to exploit any of the Ostsee's potential as a major route into Russia. There were no naval reasons for this; operations elsewhere did not really preclude much more substantial participation in the effort. Moscow was a main objective. (Note: From Leningrad, Moscow is only 400 land miles away; it lies 670 miles from the nearest land frontier, in Poland.)

Neither was the *Wehrmacht* staff sensitive to the fact that total elimination of Baltflot would in the long run have released considerable German (and Finnish) ground and air as well as naval forces for service in other areas, possibly even leading to the seizure of Murmansk and Archangel and the closure of the northern supply route.

In 1941, as a consequence, the errors of 1914 were repeated. There was no overall *joint* Army-Navy-Air Force operations plan. The Navy's capabilities remained largely unused and it assumed the strategic defensive while the Army attempted lightning offensive thrusts over vast areas with barely sufficient forces and inadequate logistic support.

In the course of the next four years, the *Wehrmacht*'s Army-centered parochial attitude and tunnel vision were to be corrected, piece by piece and at great cost. But duly corrected they were.

Even by 1944, however, the *Kriegsmarine* was a navy with a positive tradition to make for itself. The surface forces upon which so much had been lavished had signally failed (except in Norway) to achieve anything of note. The Navy was now apparently waiting hopelessly only for an ignominious repeat of 1918. Even the submarines had been too few, too late. The Navy was worth more than that.

But then, in the last days of World War II, as the Third Reich collapsed in fire and death around it, the *Kriegsmarine* earned for itself a full measure of glory. And it was this secondary Baltic theater which provided the opening to the future.

The real overall task of the German Navy by that time lay in the Baltic— no longer in the North Atlantic—supplying the desperate armies in Kurland and East Prussia and giving them supporting fire; in evacuating wounded and refugees; and finally at the end also bringing out as many of the troops themselves as it could. This was now recognized by OKW, and whatever maritime resources could be found were shifted to reflect it.

By 1944, the Navy had already suffered severe losses. There was a continual shortage of destroyers, torpedo boats, escorts, and other light craft. The Navy had always had to do without adequate air support; in the last days there was none at all. It was perennially short of fuel. The U-boat service stole all of the best and brightest young officers and men.

But in the Baltic the Navy stood and fought, and won. The subsequent evacuation of the Baltic Germans was the most important opportunity the Navy had ever been given, in all German military history.

The sheer magnitude of the evacuation makes the importance of the Navy's achievement difficult to convey. The several terrible maritime losses which punctuated the affair at almost regular intervals only cause many to blank the story out. The point is still this: despite the confusion and uncertainty which surrounded it, the German Navy accomplished more than anyone could possibly have hoped, driven by sheer moral duty. The Navy could never, under the circumstances, truly complete the work—that was beyond anyone's capability by that time.

Wars are not won with evacuations, even successful ones conducted under fire, but a worthy tradition can be. This, in the midst of immeasurable suffering, the Navy found for itself at last.

THE RECKONING

The final overall statistics on this great maritime affair are truly staggering. Overall, there were approximately 7 million refugees from the east. Involved in the Baltic evacuation were perhaps 1080 ships. They rescued a total of possibly 2,360,000 people, maybe even more. During the entire affair, some 245 merchantmen were lost. Known lost also were around 33,080 people, given as a mere 1.4 percent of those officially taken in Navy care. No one can know exactly, but when the war was over, one out of every roughly 20 free Germans was there in the west solely because of the efforts of Dönitz and his men. Even Raeder would have given a "well done."

The Handelsmarine also did itself proud. Merchant crews, fishermen, and watermen met every demand made of them. They sailed back east again and again to be filled with the homeless, the wounded, and ultimately the fleeing troops until they could find no more fuel for their ships. They ferried evacuees from shore to ship. They loaded cargo, all under fire. Voluntarily, too.

The Navy itself had to make the last runs east because only they had any fuel left. But the agony was finally over. What could be done had been done.

The war in the Baltic had indeed, however, been a unique narrow seas inshore war. The interaction between events ashore and at sea during the whole six years was direct, intense, and continuous. With the Navy, it had been somewhat less so in the early years, but as the war mounted in intensity, so was the interaction more direct, continuous in its crescendo towards the end. Here, the military position ashore determined the nature of operations at sea. Coastal, it had been, but that was not all.

Here in the Baltic, the Navy out of necessity overcame or held off some of the operational rules for war in a narrow sea. The Navy did exercise sea control, even though it never enjoyed adequate air support. It projected power ashore, relying wholly on the guns of its big ships. It protected its SLOCs, and exploited them. The Soviet air forces never prevented it from achieving any of its tasks, even during the final days. That was its glory.

It was not until the Western Allies brought their overwhelmingly superior land and air power to bear in the Baltic that the operational rules for narrow seas would be seriously felt. Continued long enough, they would no doubt have proven decisive.

The importance of smaller ships and craft—both war and merchant— which might have been slight on the open sea, was great here. The shallow Baltic was made to order for landing craft. Lighters and gun-barges were always worth their weight in gold. So were S-boats, even T-boats. So were the smaller merchantmen, motor coasters, and the like.

Aircraft and small submarines both proved useful, as we saw. Mines were the expected tremendous threat. Countermeasures soaked up equivalent numbers of always scarce assets.

THE COST

The Baltic fleet had indeed consumed itself in the process of carrying out this great maritime enterprise. The big fighting ships had done what they could, but inevitably now their time was out. British bombers sank *Admiral Scheer* in Kiel on April ninth, and her sister *Lützow* at Swinemünde on the sixteenth (*Lützow* settled on an even keel, guns still well above water, and she kept firing until she had to be blown up). Old battleships *Schleswig-Holstein* and *Schlesien* were scuttled, the first in Gotenhafen and the other in Swinemünde. *Hipper* and *Emden*, at Kiel, lay stranded, both heavily damaged by bombs. At the very end, *Prinz Eugen*, *Nürnberg*, and *Leipzig* were found in Danish ports, all that was left. Only the first two were fit for action.

Lost, too, in the Baltic were four destroyers and 12 torpedo boats. Few intact Baltic destroyers or torpedo boats fell into enemy hands.

It was the remnants of the surface fleet—manned by older and reserve personnel now, lacking the glamor and the young elite personnel of the

U-boats—that accomplished all this. More could not have been asked of them.

Under the terms of the capitulation, all shipping was to be surrendered to the Allies. Only *Prinz Eugen* and *Nürnberg* remained seaworthy enough to be sailed immediately to Wilhelmshaven, to be given up. The Baltic U-boats all scuttled, in the face of contrary orders. Since there had never been a real naval air arm, there were no planes for the Navy to give up.

When the war ended, there were still 1,300,000 tons of German merchant shipping afloat, sheltering in ports of the North Sea and the Baltic. The Swedish iron ore trade continued right down to the end. Most of the ships were otherwise no longer fit for service. One out of four had been lost.

The long line of already rusting hulks that littered the Baltic coast, blasted and burnt, masts at crazy angles, showed where most of the rest was. These blackened monuments began deep in the Finnish Gulf and ended only at Kiel.

POLITICS

Today (1989), after a history of 800 years stretching from the Christianizing knights, there are almost no more Baltic Germans in Kurland. A somewhat smaller Finland is determinedly neutral. Estonia, Latvia, and Lithuania are involuntary constituent republics of the USSR. The entire Polish nation has been shifted west, occupying East and West Prussia. Germany (what is left of it) itself is for the moment rigidly divided into east and west. The Iron Curtain runs right down the middle of what had been Hitler's Reich, splitting even Berlin. But a free prosperous Germany does exist, thanks in no small part to the lift about which we have just read.

The Germans in the east—both military and civilian—were in 1944 and 1945 only reaping at the hands of the Red Army all that Hitler had sown: torture, rape, crucifixion, individual and mass murder of all sexes and ages. Prussia was looted, stripped of everything of value. Some Russians ended up so satiated with revenge that they were sick. Degradation was repaid with degradation.

Thus, "those evacuated" *were* essentially refugees saved from Soviet terror. Wounded troops were included right from the start, of course. So were minor units cutoff and stranded on the beaches, as were selected groups of technicians, especially in the closing days. But the military were the smaller part.

Since as a rule all able-bodied males were drafted into the fighting services, and the *Wehrmacht* essentially was executing a fighting retreat south down the Kurland coast and then west back into the heart of the homeland, on land, most of the civilians rescued were in fact women, children, and old men.

Look at the numbers. Using the admittedly incomplete ones from Table 6.1, a total of 1,568,000 refugees are shown as having been brought out. The same table shows a total of 548,500 military (including wounded) were lifted out. Of the total, then, only 25 percent were combatants. For all the others, and for the wounded, this operation was a great act of mercy, from one part of a people to others.

Initially, there was some question as to whether a defeated and truncated Germany could house and feed the millions of refugees streaming back into the homeland. But a country drained of millions of its men, in chaos, soon absorbed the returnees with ease. Manpower for the sooner or later inevitable recovery was evidently going to be needed, and it was, therefore, very much welcome. The first months were the hardest. The first two winters were the worst.

This remarkable enterprise so successfully carried out cannot but also have done something to further integrate the German people. The Reich had only existed since 1871. The differences between a Rhinelander, a Prussian, and a Bavarian, for instance, still stood. With the lift, a certain additional homogenizing was bound to take place. No adult refugee could help but notice that it was a *German* Navy which saved him or her. This too was a political gain.

Germany's gut lesson in seapower—the ability to influence events at sea, and from the sea—is finished, for now. No rational German can any longer call an adequate navy a luxury. How could he, in the face of what we have just considered here?

BUNDESMARINE, NOW

Right after the war, what was still left of the *Kriegsmarine* was demolished, disbanded, or taken away. *Prinz Eugen* was claimed by the United States and destroyed during the 1946 Bikini atomic bomb tests. We received three destroyers, too. *Nürnberg* was turned over to the USSR (which renamed her *Admiral Makarov*). So were four destroyers, two torpedo boats, 42 S-boats, and nine submarines. So was badly damaged *Lützow*. The British claimed eight destroyers, four of which subsequently went to France.

Thus in the immediate postwar period, the big ships were gone. The torpedo craft were gone. Only the numerous and still extremely useful mine warfare craft remained. In the west, the British seized them, civilianized them, manned them with their ex-*Kriegsmarine* crews, and set them—under Admiralty direction—to clearing mines from the North Sea, the Baltic entrances, and the English Channel. (This was the German Mine Clearance Service [*Deutsche Minenräumdienst*]. Financial responsibility for the service seems later to have been assumed by the United

States). When in 1955 the West German government was again permitted a navy, this mine force became the principal cadre around which what was renamed the *Bundesmarine* was rebuilt.

West Germany—left with a small outlet on the Baltic (Lübeck, Kiel, and the rest of the Schleswig-Holstein coast) as well as all of Germany's prewar North Sea coast—inherits in these waters the traditional German naval role (a necessary one). Firmly committed to the Western democracies, Bonn consciously decided right from the beginning (in 1955) to integrate its limited rearmament efforts with those of the North Atlantic Treaty Organization (NATO). It thereby also acquired treaty as well as national strategic interest in the Danish Straits.

Wilhelmshaven and Kiel were redesignated the *Bundesmarine*'s main bases. To the organized civilian minesweeping cadres—and to a few civilianized S-boats similarly working (on Baltic surveillance tasks) for the British—were added five M-boats, war booty returned by France. Destroyers came from the United States, frigates (corvettes) from Britain, aircraft from both. A couple of the best of the scuttled U-boats were salvaged and refitted. The new fleet was on its way.

Today, Baltflot with its Polish and East German allies (auxiliaries) dominates the Ostsee. The Red Fleet still protects the industrial west of the USSR and the major centers at Leningrad. Baltflot at the same time provides the means to outflank West Germany, support the Red Army in its sweep into Denmark, and open the way out the Danish Straits to the North Sea and from there to the open North Atlantic. It is only 40 miles from East Germany to Denmark by sea.

The *Bundesmarine* can be classified today as a regional navy-plus, with three priority tasks. Its first priority must be defense of German coastal lines of communication, protecting its small remaining outlet on the Baltic. Its second priority involves some reach beyond immediate coastal defense, designed within coalition warfare (NATO) needs. It would cooperate closely with Denmark in holding the Straits. Last, it would contribute to NATO's other forces, as it can.

The *Bundesmarine* includes two squadrons of destroyers, and two of frigates. There are four squadrons of S-boats. There are two squadrons of submarines. Minesweepers are organized into six squadrons, forming the largest single element. The Naval Air Arm counts a reconnaissance fighter squadron, three fighter bomber squadrons, and two maritime patrol squadrons.

This Navy could draw much of its inner strength from the achievements recounted here. Its tradition it had found. It must know it.

STRIKING A BALANCE

While we are sipping our evening schnapps, or pink gin or whiskey, telling each other of the old days, it might still be worth pausing a final moment. Ghosts are watching us. That there was a massive human tragedy behind all this should be acknowledged. The 33,080 people stipulated as having died in this operation apparently just includes only those lost while in the care, ashore or afloat, of the Navy. How many died as a result of having been bombed, strafed, and shelled on the beaches, or even on the piers and quays or in the assembly areas? Or frozen? Or starved? Or been sick? No one knows.

How many waited on forgotten beaches, hiding in the wind-swept dunes, searching the Baltic's swirling mists, calling for help? Some radios lasted, others went off the air one by one as they were captured by the Soviets, their batteries ran out, or their military operators were shot. Eventually the too late, the lost, the abandoned simply drifted sadly off history's stage.

This has been an unabashedly romantic story, heavy with the old-fashioned concepts of honor and duty. It is also one full of blood, dirt and fatigue, destruction and death, burning, drowning, and typhus. For the Germans at Hela the history of World War II had come full circle. The Navy began and ended the war there.

But there is nobility in our story, too, the nobility of man rising above war. In this book I have done my best to tell it like it was, to balance some of the other things we have all heard. If there are errors, they are mine alone. All the inadequacies are mine, too. This story deserved only the best, and I trust I have served it well.

Appendixes

List of Some Key Baltic Naval Leaders

BARTELS, Heinrich (Commander). In 1944–1945; operations officer, eastern Baltic, responsible on scene during evacuation for matching ships, crews, and cargoes.

VON BLANC, Adalbert (Commander, later Rear Admiral). In 1944–1945, commanded 9th Escort Division, responsible for waters from Danzig east and north.

BURCHARDI, Theodor (Admiral). Born May 14, 1892; at beginning of war, commanding officer of light cruiser *Köln*; in January 1940, chief of staff of Naval Arsenal, Wilhelmshaven; after May 1941, commander of coastal defenses and senior naval officer, eastern Baltic. Relieved April 1945.

DÖNITZ, Karl (*Grossadmiral*). Born September 16, 1891; in April 1910, entered Navy as cadet at Kiel; in World War I, served in light cruiser *Breslau*, in U–39, as commanding officer of UC–25 and then of UC–68 until taken prisoner. Remained in Navy after war, on the naval staff, as commanding officer of torpedo boat T–157, in small cruiser *Nymphe*, as chief of 4th torpedo boat half-flotilla, and as commanding officer of light cruiser *Emden*. In 1935, chief of U-boat flotilla in Kiel. In January 1943, succeeded Raeder as commander-in-chief of the Navy; on May 1, 1945, succeeded Hitler as chief of state.

ENGELHARDT, Konrad (Captain, later Rear Admiral). Born 1899?; in 1939–1944, sea transport officer with service in France, Italy, Africa, Crimea, Baltic; in 1944–1945, *Wehrmacht* sea transport officer.

VON FRIEDEBURG, Hans-Georg (*Generaladmiral*). Born May 15, 1895; in 1937, assigned U-boat staff; in February 1943, commanding admiral of U-boats; in May 1945, Commander-in-Chief of the Navy.

HERING, Robert (Lieutenant Commander). In 1944–1945, commanding officer of torpedo boat T–36.

HEYDAL, Hugo (Commander). In 1944–1945, commanded 10th Escort Division, responsible for the western Baltic.

KLOSE, Hans-Helmut (Lieutenant Commander). In March 1945, commanded S-boats at Libau.

KUMMETZ, Oscar (*Generaladmiral*). Born July 21, 1891; in October 1939, chief of staff of the fleet, then inspector of torpedo forces; in 1940, commander of task force Oslo; later commander of cruisers, then commander of a battle group in northern Norway; in March 1944, Commander-in-Chief, Baltic.

LANGE, Werner (Vice Admiral). Commander of coastal defenses and senior naval officer, western Baltic. Relieved March 1945.

LEONHARDT, Wolfgang (Lieutenant Commander). In 1944–1945, operations officer of 9th Escort Division, at Danzig.

ROGGE, Bernhard (Vice Admiral). Born November 4, 1899; commanding officer of auxiliary cruiser (raider) *Atlantis*; near end of war, organized and led battle group "Rogge," fighting in the east.

SCHEUERLEN, Ernst (Vice Admiral). Commander of 2nd Naval Infantry Division; killed in action on eastern front.

SCHMALENBACH, Paul (Lieutenant Commander). In 1944, developed joint gunfire support system for Force 2.

THIELE, August (Vice Admiral). Born August 26, 1893; commanding officer of armored cruiser *Lützow*; in April 1940, commandant Trondheim; Admiral Norwegian north coast; in August 1941, chief of staff of fleet; in Juy 1944, organized Force 2 for duty in the Baltic; in April 1945, senior naval officer, eastern Baltic.

Glossary of Foreign Terms

Baltenflotte	German Baltic Fleet 1941
Baltflot	Soviet Baltic Fleet in WWII
Bundesmarine	German Navy 1955 to present
Deutsche Minenräum-dienst	German Mine Clearance Service
Estland	Estonia
Fährprahm	Self-propelled ferry-barge (F-lighter)
Festung	Fortress
Fish Cutter	German utility boat (trawler hull)
Führer	Leader (Hitler)
Gauleiter	Area Party Leader
Handelsmarine	German Merchant Marine
Imperial Marine	German Navy 1871–1918
Kriegsmarine	German Navy 1935–1945
Kurland	Courland (Eastern Baltic Coast)
Lettland	Latvia
Luftwaffe	German Air Force 1935–1945
Marineoberkommando, Ostsee (MOK Ost)	Naval High Commander, Baltic

Oberkommando der Marine (OKM)	Navy Headquarters/high command
Oberkommando der Wehrmacht	Armed Forces Headquarters
Ostland	Eastern Baltic
Ostsee	Baltic Sea
Reichsmarine	German Navy 1919–1934
Reikosee	Reich Commissioner for Shipping
Schnellboot	German motor torpedo boat
Second Reich	Weimar Republic
Seekriegsleitung (SKL)	Navy Operations Staff
Seetra	Wehrmacht Sea Transport Office(r)
Siebelfähre	Self-propelled lighter
Sperrbrecher	Magnetic Mine Clearance Vessel
Third Reich	Hitler's Germany
Torpedo Cutter	Soviet motor torpedo boat
Volk	Folk, people
Wehrmacht	German Armed Forces 1935–1945

Military Abbreviations and Acronyms

AA	Antiaircraft
ASW	Antisubmarine warfare
GRT	Gross registered ton (measurement for merchantmen; the Navy uses displacement ton)
KFK	Fishcutter
KMD	Naval service field office
M-boat	Minesweeper
ME–262	Jet-powered German fighter plane
MFP	Naval ferry-barge (F-lighter)
MOK Ost	Naval group command, Baltic
ObdM	Commander-in-Chief, Navy
OKM	Navy Headquarters
OKW	Armed Forces Headquarters
RAF	(British) Royal Air Force
R-boat	Motor minesweeper
Reikosee	Reich commissioner for shipping
S-boat	Motor torpedo boat (*Schnellboot*)
Seetra	Wehrmacht sea transport officer
SKL	Navy operations staff
T-boat	Torpedo boat

U-boat	Submarine
V–1	Ramjet-powered subsonic missile (flying bomb)
V–2	Rocket-powered ballistic missile
Z-boat	Destroyer

Appendix A
Typical Characteristics of Key Ships: Cruisers

	Armored Cruisers	Heavy Cruisers	Light Cruisers
Displacement: normal (tons)	11,700	14,000	6,650
max	16,000	18,000	8,200
Speed: max/cruise (knots)	28/20	32/20	32/19
Range (seamiles)	9,000	6,800	5,700
Armament: 11-inch	6 (2 x 3)		
8-inch		8	
5.9-inch			9 (Emden 8)
4.1-inch	6	12	
3.5-inch			6
37-mm	8	12	8
20-mm	28	28	10
torpedo tubes	8	12	12
Designation	Lützow	Prinz Eugen	Nürnberg
	Admiral Scheer	Admiral Hipper	Leipzig
			Köln
			Emden

Appendix B
Fate of Major *Ostsee* Ships, Spring 1945

Type	Name	History
Armored cruiser	Lützow	Bombed April 16 at Swindemunde; sank on even keel, continued firing; blown up May 4
	Admiral Scheer	Bombed, capsized at Kiel April 9/10
Heavy cruiser	Admiral Hipper	Bombed at Kiel, blown up May 3
	Prinz Eugen	Took refuge in Copenhagen
Light cruiser	Emden	Blown up at Kiel in April
	Leipzig	Damaged, took refuge in Apenrade
Old battleships	Schleswig-Holstein	Damaged by bombs in Gotenhafen in December, sank on even keel, continued firing, abandoned January 25
	Schlesien	Blown up May 4 at Swinemünde

Appendix C
Typical Characteristics of Key Ships: Torpedo Craft

	Destroyers	Torpedo Boats	Motor Torpedo Boats
Displacement: normal (tons)	2,600	850/1,400	95/105
max	3,600	1,000/1,800	
Speed: max/cruise (knots)	36/19	34/19	39
Range (seamiles)	6,000	2,500	700
Armament:			
5.9-inch	5		
4.1-inch		4	
37-mm	4	4	1?
20-mm	14	7/12	2?
torpedo tubes	8	6	2
mines	60	40/50	6
Designation	Z-numbers	T-boats	S-boats
	Some (not all)		
	also have names.		
	"Z-boats"		

Appendix D
Torpedo Boat Losses

T-number	Date, Location, and Cause of Loss
T-3	March 14, 1945, north of Hela by a mine
T-5	March 14, 1945, east of Hela by a mine
T-8	May 3, 1945, near Kiel, bombed
T-9	May 3, 1945, near Kiel, bombed
T-10	December 18, 1944, in Gotenhafen dock, bombed
T-18	September 17, 1944, northwest of Balticport, bombed and strafed
T-22	August 18, 1944, in Finnish Gulf by a mine
T-30	August 18, 1944, in Finnish Gulf by a mine
T-31	June 20, 1944, in Finnish Gulf, torpedoed by a torpedo cutter
T-32	August 18, 1944, in Finnish Gulf, by a mine
T-34	November 20, 1944, east of Arkona by a mine
T-36	May 4, 1945, in central Baltic, bombed and mined

Total: 12 torpedo boats

Note: T-13, 16, 17, 19, 20, 21, 23, 28, 33, 35, 108, T-*Löwe*, and T-*Panther* all served in the area and appear to have survived the war.

Appendix E
Typical Characteristics of Key Ships: Mine Warfare Craft

	Minesweepers	Motor Minesweepers
Displacement: normal (tons)	540/680	125
max	770/880	20
Speed (knots)	16/18	
Range (seamiles)	4,000	900
Armament:		
4.1-inch	1/2	
37-mm	2	3/6
20-mm	8	1/4
mines	24/30	12
Designation	M-boats	R-boats

Appendix F
Merchant Ships Lost—by Cause—1944–1945 in Baltic

	Mines	Torpedoes	Bombs	Gunfire	Scuttling	Capture	Total
Jan-Dec 1944	29	7	42	3	3		84
Jan-Dec 1945	44	10	88	2	4	12	161
Total	73	17	130	5	7	12	245
Jan 1945	8	1	2	1			12
Feb 1945	10	3	3				17*
Mar 1945	17	3	12		2	2	36
Apr 1945	6	3	37	1	2	2	51
May 1945	3		34			8	45
Total	44	10	88	2	4	12	161

*Includes one ship lost through collision, not listed above.
Source: Heniz Schön, *Ostsee '45.*

Appendix G
Merchant Ships Lost—by Tonnage and Personnel

	Number	Tonnage (GRT)		People	
Jan–Dec 1944	84	179,220		1,903	
Jan–Dec 1945	161	559,565		31,179	
Total	245	738,785		33,082	
Jan 1945	12	60,710		5,990	?
Feb 1945	17	59,155		5,109	
Mar 1945	36	116,823		1,261	
Apr 1945	51	159,967		10,555	?
May 1945	45	162,910	?	8,264	
Total	161	559,565		31,179	

Source: Heinz Schön, *Ostsee '45*.

Bibliography

There is not a lot easily available on this subject for those who would read more. Of those books most easily accessible to readers in English, most are useful only for background, dealing with the evacuation in only a paragraph or two. The following seem most worthwhile:

Bekker, Cajus. *Defeat at Sea*. New York: Ballantine Books, 1953. Two good chapters on the Baltic.

———. *Flucht übers Meer*. Oldenburg: Gerhard Stalling Verlag, 1959. Also Frankfurt/M: Ullstein Buch, 1976.

———. *Hitler's Naval War*. Frank Ziegler, trans. and ed. Garden City, NY: Doubleday, 1974. Background.

Bennett, Geoffrey. *Cowan's War*. London: Collins, 1964.

Brice, Martin. *Axis Blockade Runners of World War II*. London: B. T. Batsford, 1981.

Brustat-Naval, Fritz. *Unternehmen Rettung*. Herford: Koehler Verlagsgesellschaft, 1970. Includes commentary from Admiral Engelhardt.

Dobson, Christopher, John Miller, and Ronald Payne. *The Cruellest Night*. London: Hodder and Stoughton, 1979. A newsman's account, but full of interesting data and human-interest stories.

Dönitz, Karl. *Deutsche Strategie zur See im Zweiten Weltkrieg*. Munich and Frankfurt/M: Bernard and Graefe, 1969 and 1972.

———. *10 Jahre und 20 Tage*. Frankfurt/M: Athenäum, 1958. Also in English as *Memoirs*. London: Weidenfeld and Nicolson, 1959.

Fredmann, Ernst. *Sie kamen übers Meer*. Cologne: SWG, 1971.

Groner, Erich. *Die Deutschen Kriegschiffe*. 6 vols; Koblenz: Bernard & Graefe Verlag, 1982–. Not yet completed.

Güth, Rolf. *Die Marine des Deutschen Reiches 1919–1939*. Munich: Bernard & Graefe Verlag, 1972. The interwar navy.

Herwig, Holger H. *"Luxury" Fleet*. London: George Allen & Unwin, 1980. The Kaiser's navy.

Horn, Daniel. *The German Naval Mutinies of World War I*. New Brunswick, NJ: Rutgers University Press, 1969.

Kühn, Volkmar. *Torpedoboote und Zerstörer im Einsatz 1939–1945*. Stuttgart: Motorbuch Verlag, 1983.

Lass, Edgar Gunther. *Die Flucht, Ostpreussen 1944–1945*. Bad Nauheim: Podzun-Verlag, 1964.

Lüdde-Neurath, W. *Regierung Dönitz*. Göttingen: Musterschmidt, 1953.

Mallmann-Schowell, J. P. *Das Buch der Deutschen Kriegsmarine 1935–1945*. Stuttgart: Motorbuch Verlag, 1987.

Martienssen, Anthony. *Hitler and His Admirals*. New York: E. P. Dutton & Co., 1949. Interesting, different.

Meister, J. *Der Seekrieg in osteuropäischen Gewassern 1941–1945*. Munich: Lehmanns, 1958.

Padfield, Peter. *Dönitz, the last Führer*. London: Panther, 1985. A readable account of the life of the man behind it all.

Prager, Hans-Georg. *Panzerschiff "Deutschland"/Schwerer Kreuzer "Lützow."* Herford: Koehlers Verlag, 1981.

Ruge, Friedrich. *Der Seekrieg*. M. G. Saunders, trans. Annapolis, MD: U.S. Naval Institute, 1957. Background.

———. *Im Küstenvorfield*. Munich: Bernard & Graefe Verlag, 1977. Inshore warfare.

———. *Scapa Flow 1919*. Derek Masters, trans., A. J. Watts, ed. London: Ian Allen, 1973.

———. *The Soviets as Naval Opponents 1941–1945*. Annapolis, MD: U.S. Naval Institute, 1979.

Salewski, Michael. *Die Deutsche Seekriegsleitung 1935–1945*, 3 vols. Munich: Bernard & Graefe, 1975. The authoritative work.

Schmalenbach, Paul. *Kreuzer "Prinz Eugen."* Herford: Koehlers Verlag, 1978. By her gunnery officer.

Schön, Heinz. *Flucht über die Ostsee*. Stuttgart: Motorbuch Verlag, 1985. Pictorial.

———. *Ostsee '45*. Stuttgart: Motorbuch Verlag, 1985. An exhaustive work, full of technical detail, in German.

Van der Vat, Dan. *The Grand Scuttle*. Annapolis, MD: U.S. Naval Institute Press, 1986.

Whitley, M. J. *Destroyer*. Annapolis: U.S. Naval Institute, 1983.

Witthöft, Hans-Jürgen. *Hansa-Bauprogramm*. Munich: Bernard & Graefe Verlag, 1975. The merchant war emergency building program.

Index

ABOUT THE AUTHOR

CHARLES W. KOBURGER, Jr. is a Captain in the U.S. Coast Guard Reserve, retired in 1978 after 20 years active duty. He is now an independent consultant in the operational aspects of maritime affairs, specializing in navigation systems. Holder of masters degrees in political science and history, he is also a 1965 graduate of the Armed Forces Staff College. In 1983–84, he was the Sir John Cass Fellow at the City of London Polytechnic, working on vessel traffic systems. He has been published professionally many times on both sides of the Atlantic. He is the author of *Sea Power in the Falklands* (Praeger, 1983) and *Vessel Traffic Systems. The Cyrano Fleet* (Praeger) appeared in 1989.